ONE STEP AT A TIME

D0311463

THOMAS NELSON PUBLISHERS
Nashville
❖ *A Janet Thoma Book* ❖

❖ *A Janet Thoma Book* ❖

Published in Nashville, Tennessee, by Thomas Nelson, Inc., and distributed in Canada by Lawson Falle, Ltd., Cambridge, Ontario.

Scripture quotations are from the NEW KING JAMES VERSION of the Bible. Copyright © 1979, 1980, 1982, Thomas Nelson, Inc., Publishers.

Library of Congress Cataloging-in-Publication Data

Minirth, Frank B.
    One step at a time / Frank Minirth, Betty Blaylock, Cynthia Humbert.
        p.   cm. — (Serenity meditation series)
    ISBN 0-8407-3339-9 (pbk.)
    1. Twelve-step programs—Religious aspects—Meditations.   I. Blaylock, Betty.   II. Humbert, Cynthia.   III. Title.   IV. Series.
BL624.5.M57   1991
242'.4—dc20   91-30796
                                         CIP

Printed in the United States of America
1 2 3 4 5 6 7 — 96 95 94 93 92 91

Acknowledgments

The authors are grateful to friends, family members, and working companions whose contributions and assistance have made this publication possible. We are especially thankful to Charles C. Blaylock, David Humbert, and Michal and Wayne Spell for their encouragement and support; to Kathy Barnes, Dick Blaylock, Suzy Blaylock, Jeanie Connell, Kit Fensterbush, Ron Harris, Pat Little, Jane Mack, Janet Reynolds, Myrna Thompson, Donna Tillinghast, and George Weir for writing contributions, and to Betty McNalley and Judy Huemmer for their hours of typing; and Janet Thoma and Susan Salmon for their editorial expertise.

Finally, we would like to express appreciation to the counselees we have worked with through the years, especially those touched by a history in dysfunctional families. We hope the experiences shared will bring a clearer understanding of the dynamics of a Twelve Step program and how change can be brought about in your own life, one step at a time.

The Twelve Steps of Alcoholics Anonymous

1. We admitted we were powerless over alcohol—that our lives had become unmanageable.
2. Came to believe that a Power greater than ourselves could restore us to sanity.
3. Made a decision to turn our will and our lives over to the care of God as we understood Him.
4. Made a searching and fearless moral inventory of ourselves.
5. Admitted to God, to ourselves and to another human being the exact nature of our wrongs.
6. Were entirely ready to have God remove all these defects of character.
7. Humbly asked Him to remove our shortcomings.
8. Made a list of all persons we had harmed and became willing to make amends to them all.
9. Made direct amends to such people wherever possible, except when to do so would injure them or others.
10. Continued to take personal inventory and when we were wrong, promptly admitted it.
11. Sought through prayer and meditation to improve our conscious contact with God, as we understood Him, praying only for knowledge of His will for us and the power to carry that out.
12. Having had a spiritual awakening as the result of these steps, we tried to carry this message to alcoholics, and to practice these principles in all our affairs.

Introduction

Frank Minirth, as cofounder of the Minirth-Meier Clinic, and Betty Blaylock and I, as counselors with the Clinic, have seen hundreds of people's lives changed as a result of their participation in a Twelve-Step recovery program.

Through counseling and research, we have gained insight into the many "roles" people learn that are not balanced, healthy, or comfortable. And as we have been committed to integrating the truth of God's Word with sound psychological principles, we have seen men and women from abusive and dysfunctional families accept their pasts and begin to live emotionally and spiritually healthy lives.

Betty has counseled particularly extensively with adult children of alcoholics and helped them find love, determination, and faith in God's will that has led them to the path of healing and happiness. And in my counseling with adults and adolescents, I have seen therapy provide courage and truth for people facing issues of codependency, post-abortion trauma, and depression.

In the following pages, you will walk through one step of the Twelve Steps each month, starting with Step One. It is our desire that, with the help of these Twelve Steps, you will be able to identify and overcome your own painful memories and behaviors and understand that change is possible as you yield to the grace of God in Christ.

God bless you,

Cynthia Spell Humbert
Minirth-Meier Clinic

*We admitted we were powerless over our
dependencies—that our lives had become
unmanageable.*

Many times we ignore the physical symptoms that
tell us we have a serious problem. Headaches, skin
rashes, stomachaches, and pain in our jaws can all be
physical symptoms of repressed anger, fear, and guilt.

Another form of denial is not admitting that a problem is very serious. A friend's daughter has tried to
commit suicide two times; her parents attribute it to
stress over final exams. Their denial is in not looking at
the seriousness of the root problem.

Blaming something or someone else is a good way
to deny our responsibility in the problem. "It's your
fault I drink. You spend too much money, the house is a
mess, and you can't cook anything worth eating." We
also deny by changing the subject if the topic becomes
threatening or becoming angry in order to avoid the
issue.

What form does your denial take? Are you ready to
admit that you are powerless over changing yourself,
without help from someone else? You can only get help
by asking in an open and honest way.

Pride is only a security blanket for low self-esteem.

BLB

Old habits die hard.
—ANONYMOUS

Our old habits and behavior patterns may easily return if we are not careful to monitor them. Some of our habits were like dear friends to us. Our dependencies created more chaos in our lives, but we developed our habits as reactions to the stressors we faced.

We need to realize how easily we could return to these dangerous coping mechanisms when we feel pressured. We need to monitor our actions and watch for self-destructive behavior. Sponsors in Twelve-Step programs help keep us accountable. We all need the support of someone who can view us in an unbiased, objective way. Working the program with a group also provides a good way to receive feedback.

Once we admit that we are powerless, we begin to seek God for guidance. He brings order to the chaos caused by our addictions. By seeking God's guidance and by learning from other people in recovery, we can develop healthy ways to cope with the stresses of life.

Admitting we are powerless is not a defeat; it is the first step toward a victory.

CSH

> *But I discipline my body and bring it into*
> *subjection, lest, when I have preached to others,*
> *I myself should become disqualified.*
>   —1 COR. 9:27

We do not have to go out and look for temptation. It never leaves our side. It gets in front of us to make us stumble or pushes us from behind. The Lord even instructed us to pray, "lead us not into temptation." Basically, temptation is that little voice inside our head that says, "Go ahead and do it," when we know we should not.

The Bible tells us stories of people who gave in to temptation. In Genesis, Eve was tempted to eat the forbidden fruit. Satan promised her that if she did, she would be like God.

Jesus was also tempted. In Matthew, we see him in the wilderness dealing with the same temptations that we deal with every day. The first temptation attacked his physical hunger. He was tempted to use his power to satisfy his own physical needs. The second temptation enticed Jesus to seek recognition for himself. The third temptation was for Jesus to worship false gods. The real issue here is, who is going to be lord of our life? Is it alcohol, sex, food, money, or another person?

Recognize temptation, and realize the power of the Lord to overcome it. Read the Word of God for strength to withstand temptation.

                                                          BLB

Then He arose and rebuked the wind, and said to the sea, "Peace, be still!" And the wind ceased and there was a great calm.   —MARK 4:39

The Gospel of Mark gives an account of Jesus and his disciples sailing in a boat during a great windstorm. The storm increased, large waves crashed against the boat, and water flooded over the sides of their small craft, yet Jesus slept through this frightening storm. They awakened him and said, "Teacher, do you not care that we are perishing?" Responding quickly, Jesus verbally rebuked the wind and told the sea to be at peace. The storm ceased and the sea grew calm.

The disciples certainly felt powerless during that storm. They felt overwhelmed and feared that Jesus didn't really care about their safety. All they needed to do was ask Jesus, and he took control of the situation.

Often we behave like these disciples because our fear and lack of trust increase our feelings of being out of control. We create our own stormy sea experience through our dependencies. Then, attempting to rescue ourselves, we lean more heavily on our addictions.

We find hope in knowing that Jesus promises to bring us peace when we place our faith in him. He is the one person who is always trustworthy.

God is able to calm our fears and teach us to trust again.

CSH

> *"Be angry, and do not sin": do not let the sun go*
> *down on your wrath, nor give place to the devil.*
> —EPH. 4:26–27

God permits anger, but he also tells us to direct it at sin, not at the sinner. Living with the disease of alcoholism creates many opportunities for us to become angry. Most of the anger is at ourselves because we feel so out of control. But often we get into trouble when we project our anger onto those we love. Being angry at them only pushes them away and isolates us, when what we really need is their love and support.

How can we constructively deal with our own anger? We need to deal with it quickly and fairly and then let it go. First, we should learn about the disease of alcoholism and the relationship it has with anger. Learning the causes and cures helps us put a label on what we are fighting. Secondly, we need to look at ourselves. If we are in denial, we are stuffing our anger. Third, we need to separate our anger from the disease of alcoholism, so that we can attack the repressed anger in a constructive way.

God loves the sinner but hates the sin.

BLB

I am weary with my groaning;
All night I make my bed swim;
I drench my couch with my tears.
—PS. 6:6

As we begin recovery, we must recognize the areas of our lives that have caused us the most sadness. We must admit defeat and realize our need for God's help.

In Step One we admit that our dependencies have crippled us. Our addiction cycle has made us powerless over our own behavior. Until we admit that our life has become unmanageable, we remain caught by our addictions. We need to learn to let go, to surrender ourselves to God.

We may need to take an inventory of the price we have paid for our addiction. It is helpful to compile a list of the losses we and others have suffered because of our obsessive traits. In making our list we may become aware of losses we had not considered before, such as violation of intimacy in relationships, poor work performance, or inner pain due to separation from God.

Once we recognize the pain and grief of our losses we can surrender to the fact that we are powerless. Yielding our broken lives to God will allow him to restore us to a spiritual relationship so we can begin the process of healing.

Lord, take me, mold me, and make me after your will.

CSH

Now the Lord is the Spirit; and where the Spirit of
the Lord is, there is liberty.   —2 COR. 3:17

Have you ever felt disappointed because something did not meet your expectations? Maybe you wanted a bicycle for Christmas and didn't get one. Maybe you ordered a shirt by mail and the company substituted another color. Or maybe you had settled into your home and your spouse's company decided to transfer you to another city. All these circumstances make us feel powerless and bring on feelings of disappointment.

Sometimes we disappoint ourselves. We cannot meet our own expectations, so we get discouraged and lose confidence. Then we often try to put the blame on others. We blame our spouse, our parents, our children, our boss. We become bitter and sink lower into the depths of despair.

God can give us the power to overcome and the ability to be content.
He is always there for us.

BLB

You are exactly where God wants you to be.
—ANONYMOUS

Our society tells us that our value equals what we achieve, so we look outside ourselves for our self-worth. We shift from competing for grades and sports recognition in school to competing in the business world as adults. Our accomplishments become the measure of our success.

We start to feel great anxiety and stress as we classify ourselves as either winners or losers. Increasingly we base our self-esteem and worth on our jobs, our material possessions, our social position, and what other people think of us, instead of on our internal value.

This behavior is like the frustration of building sand castles. They require lots of creative energy and time, but eventually they crumble and wash away. Basing our self-esteem on events outside ourselves may take years of planning and hard work, yet the result is nothing.

———————

Accepting powerlessness leads to the freedom to regain your self-esteem from the inside out, instead of trying to create it externally through performance.

CSH

> *"It is written in the Prophets, 'And they shall all be taught by God.' Therefore everyone who has heard and learned from the Father comes to Me."*
> —JOHN 6:45

Our perception of God is based on many experiences and relationships. Also, our perception is probably based on how we were treated by someone who was expected to love us.

Dr. Spock told parents how to hold their babies, when to feed them, and what to feed them. Problems could be solved by just reading what Dr. Spock said. His book became the child-rearing bible of the twentieth century.

The fact is, though, it was not the Bible. More than two thousand years ago the Bible told us to love one another and how to do it. It described the way parents should speak and behave toward their children, and it also told how children should speak and behave toward their parents. The Bible also spoke of a loving Father who was always there, was always forgiving, and loved us unconditionally.

As we learn to live in a healthy way, let us go to God for instruction.

_____

Hold close to your heart the love of God. Let go of the traits that hurt you.

BLB

Pain cannot be measured or compared, but we can all agree that it hurts.   —JANET REYNOLDS

After Daisy attended her first Twelve-Step meeting, she walked away with the attitude that the dysfunction of her family was not as severe as the families of everyone else in the meeting. Unfortunately, Daisy was able to deny the seriousness of her own problems and her need for help by focusing on others who had experienced more abuse than she had. Many of us deny our problems just like Daisy.

Maybe we never used mood-altering substances, but have we explored the subtle ways we avoid our feelings? We may bury ourselves in work or church or become dependent on relationships or compulsive behaviors to try to ease the anxieties and insecurities that exist in our lives.

We must recognize that we are powerless and our lives have become unmanageable. Once we see that even our "subtle" problems are serious, we can ask for help and receive it.

———————————

Denial keeps us from pursuing new life through recovery.

CSH

*I can do all things through Christ who strengthens
me.*   —PHIL. 4:13

Last fall I was given a job to do at our church. At the
time I had serious doubts about my ability to do the
job. At first I thought I was too old; then I doubted I had
enough experience to handle the job.

I was in a Bible study at the time and we were study-
ing Genesis. We had just reached the part where Abraham and Sarah were struggling with the jobs God was
giving them. Just when Abraham and Sarah doubted
that God would ever fulfill his promise of a child, Sarah
found out she was going to have a baby. She cried out,
"Get a younger person. I'm too old for the job," and
added, "I don't know if I can do a good job of being a
mother this late in life."

Sarah had given up on God once before and taken
the job of providing Abraham with a son into her own
hands. She thought she could handle the job without
him. Now here he was, giving her a second chance to
do something special for him.

_____

*When God gives us a job to do, he also provides the power to get the
job done.*

                                                      BLB

*"And he would gladly have filled his stomach with
the pods that the swine ate, and no one gave him
anything."*
                                    —LUKE 15:16

Jesus told a parable where the younger of two sons
asked for his inheritance, left his home and his father,
and wasted his wealth on riotous living. He found himself in a land full of famine and took a job feeding pigs.
Hunger so overwhelmed him that he wanted the food
the pigs ate.

To fully understand this situation, we need to remember that pigs were an unclean animal to the Jews.
It degraded the young man to touch a pig, but it was
even worse to long for the food of pigs. The prodigal
son had hit bottom.

The son remembered that his father's servants ate
plenty, so he decided to return home and ask for help.
The father saw him coming and ran out to meet him.
The father refused to disinherit his son, but rather prepared a feast to celebrate his return.

This is a wonderful example of grace. Just like the
prodigal son, we once rebelled and practiced self-
centered behaviors. God continues to show a loving attitude toward us even though we once turned our
backs on him. He waits for us to realize that we are
powerless and return home to him.

I rejoice that God's grace brought me into the program.

                                                    CSH

> *"Martha, Martha, you are worried and troubled*
> *about many things. But one thing is needed, and*
> *Mary has chosen that good part, which will not be*
> *taken away from her."*   —LUKE 10:41–42

I worried through my school days, early marriage years, and while my children were growing up, and now I have grandchildren to worry about. Over all these years, little of what I worried about ever happened. Jesus said, "Do not worry about your life, what you will eat or what you will drink; nor about your body, what you will put on" (Matt. 6:25). Why do we worry? We choose not to believe in God.

Worry creates tension, stress, isolation, and doubt in your life. Worry impairs your decision-making ability and makes you incapable of handling life's problems. You could even say, "I am powerless over worry. My mind is so preoccupied with worry that my life is unmanageable."

Martha worried because she had so much work to do and her sister Mary was not helping. Mary sat at Jesus' feet, taking in every word. Jesus told Martha not to worry and to sit down with the rest of them and hear about God.

When we pray rather than worry, we receive the peace that passes all understanding.

BLB

The will of God will never take you where the grace
of God will not protect you.   —ANONYMOUS

I often say that therapy is like going to the doctor and hearing that your appendix is abscessed. At that point, you have two choices. One is to refuse surgery, which would allow the appendix to rupture and would lead to death. The other is to have the appendix removed. Not such a tough decision, you say. Well, what if the doctor has informed you that there will be no anesthesia during surgery, so the pain will be extreme. Therefore, both options will be very painful.

Many of us make the first choice when we remain in the pain of our addictions. Recovery is a form of emotional surgery where we seek to remove the festering wounds from our hearts. Cleaning out those wounds will be painful, but it will lead us to a place of healing.

Both options are painful. Refusing recovery leads to continuing pain, but accepting the challenge of recovery leads to a healthier life. Since we realize our future will be painful, it seems wise to choose a positive form of pain that will lead to healing.

Recognizing pain and admitting that we are powerless allows us to choose life.

CSH

*No temptation has overtaken you except such as is
common to man; but God is faithful, who will not
allow you to be tempted beyond what you are able,
but with the temptation will also make the way of
escape, that you may be able to bear it.*
—1 COR. 10:13

Many times we fall down under the burden of our problems. The load feels too heavy to carry alone; this heaviness is a feeling of depression.

Peter felt deep depression after he denied the Lord. The Bible tells us that when he was reminded of his denial, he went out alone and wept. When our sense of failure becomes such a heavy burden that we sink into depression, no home remedy is going to cure it. Often we look for a way of escape. We think there is power in pills, alcohol, food, and money. We reach out and grasp those things, hoping their power will lift our burdens. In fact, they only create more problems.

Did you know that God has provided ways for us to deal with our problems? The power for healing is Jesus Christ. When we ask him to come into our life and heal us, the depression lifts, the problems are solvable, and we experience the undeserved love of God.

People often forget that God is the power that overcomes depression.
BLB

*In dysfunctional families, the individual exists to
keep the system in balance.*
　　　　　　　　　—JOHN BRADSHAW

The old Mighty Mouse cartoon's theme song proclaimed, "Here he comes to save the day." It is only
natural for us to have some reaction to growing up in a
dysfunctional family. Some of us became the hero of
the family in order to give the system some dignity. We
practice being a super-hero so often that we may as
well get a leotard and cape in order to complete our
identity! Always on the lookout for someone in distress
who needs to be rescued, much of our self-esteem
comes from our idea that we are capable of "saving the
day" for other people.

Acting as a hero may get us pats on the back, but it
keeps us from having our own needs met. We expend
so much energy taking care of others that we never
learn how to take care of ourselves.

Heroes have a tough time admitting their powerlessness, because the act of rescuing feels powerful. Often
heroes must burn out before they reach an intolerable
level of pain and take the first step toward allowing
God to be God and save the day.

_____

*We must realize that we are powerless before we can surrender
to God.*

　　　　　　　　　　　　　　　　　　　　CSH

*For I say, through the grace given to
me, to everyone who is among you, not to think of
himself more highly than he ought to think,
but to think soberly, as God has dealt to
each one a measure of faith.*   —ROM. 12:3

When our personal identity is attacked as a child, we grow up with a distorted self-image. We either have a very low self-image, feeling that we are less than others, or we have a very grandiose image of ourselves, thinking that we are better than other people. We call this feeling of self-importance pride.

There are two sides to pride. One side refers to dignity and self-respect. When our opinion of ourselves becomes inflated, then pride allows us to think too highly of our own ability. It even leads us to think we are capable of living our life without the power of God.

Pride interferes with our ability to see things as they really are. It blocks our ability to have concern for the other person. Pride makes us powerless, because we depend on self-power rather than God-power.

God can return us to healthy thinking. God loves us and needs us to do his will on earth.

Healthy self-esteem allows us to be who God wants us to be, no better, no less than anyone else.

BLB

> *The first mile of a long journey begins with a single step.*
> —LAO TZU

A fighter pilot is taught how to manage his aircraft during a dogfight. Pilots come to believe that there is no situation which cannot be overcome. Air Force psychologists report that the hardest thing to teach the pilots is when to admit that their situation has become unmanageable and bail out.

Although our daily lives may not be filled with such life-or-death decisions, it seems that, like the fighter pilot, the most difficult thing for us to do is confess our helplessness.

Allen recently went through the pain of divorce. After his wife left, he tried everything to get her back. Nothing worked. He really believed he could manage the unmanageable, but he finally accepted that he could not "save the plane from going down."

Knowing and admitting that he was powerless to change the events of the divorce did not make the pain and anxiety go away. However, it allowed God to show his unlimited grace. Allen had taken the first step.

God is patiently waiting for us to turn over control to him.

CSH

*Knowledge puffs up, but love edifies. And if anyone
thinks that he knows anything, he knows nothing
yet as he ought to know. But if anyone loves God,
this one is known by Him.*   1 COR. 8:1–3

The hardest thing to do is to admit that we are power-less over someone else, or over our own behavior or emotions. We seek help from friends, ministers, and counselors, hoping they will have the magic formula to help us feel better. Gene Gordon, a Methodist minister, has counseled more than two thousand recovering alcoholics. Gene tells his story of how he grew up on the streets as a teenager without parental supervision. His grandmother came and got him when he was fourteen and tried to help him straighten out his life. The love she had for Gene pulled him through his teenage years. Today, through love, he helps others.

We often make excuses: We would be happy if we had married or had not married. We would be wealthier if our boss hadn't given the job to someone else. We would be better equipped for close relationships if our parents had shown us love and understanding. No matter how hard we seek happiness, we will not find peace until we ask God to change our heart and we accept the things we cannot change.

We create our own misery. We can choose to concentrate on the problem or to let it go.

BLB

A man should never be ashamed to own he has
been in the wrong, which is but saying, in other
words, that he is wiser today than he was yesterday.
      —ALEXANDER POPE

Hitting bottom in at least one aspect of life led us to seek help. When we joined a Twelve Step support group, we soon realized that our lives were affected in many areas. Gradually, as we became aware of these unmanageable areas, we found a release, a freedom, and a new strength through admitting that we had no control over our addictions.

Taking Step One is not a one-time event. In each individual problem area, we find ourselves trying to grab the reins of control again and again. Each time we seek control we face the pain of failure, and we must again admit our powerlessness and submit our will to God.

It is encouraging to realize that these "failures" are actually rungs on the ladder of success. Often we learn real spiritual truths through the pain of what looks like a failure. Our successes come when we submit to God and allow him to control the process of our recovery.

Practicing this powerlessness on a moment-by-moment basis helps us learn to give up our own self-will and submit to God's will.

                                  CSH

Turn Yourself to me, and have mercy on me,
For I am desolate and afflicted.
                                        —PS. 25:16

The Bible is full of accounts of people who struggled to overcome the weaknesses of human nature. Adam tasted the fruit of the tree of good and evil and God drove him from the Garden. From Abraham's sin came Ishmael, the father of the Arab nation. On and on we see the struggle people went through and the consequences they faced for their actions. God had to teach them that they did not have complete power over their own lives, just as he teaches us.

Many of us feel we are in control of our lives until uncontrollable events begin to happen—a serious or life-threatening illness, a layoff at work, or the end of an important friendship. In trying to cope we sometimes turn to alcohol, tranquilizers, or food to comfort ourselves. Sometimes we use other means like burying ourselves in work, church activities, or relationships. We seem to go around and around emotionally like riding on a merry-go-round. When we get tired and want to get off, we realize we do not have the power to do this. Surrendering to this sense of powerlessness is not easy, but it is a beginning.

There is a miracle in every new beginning (Herman Hesse).

                                                    BLB

We can be positive that our active addiction was
negative.
                                              —ANONYMOUS

Six Flags over Texas claims to have the world's largest wooden roller coaster. The vast arrangement of razor-sharp turns, steep elevations, and plummeting drops on the ride creates a feeling of daring and excitement. Yet consider the reason most roller-coaster rides only last for a few minutes.

Those first few minutes are thrilling, but imagine how your body would react to a full hour on the roller coaster. Excitement changes to fear and dread as the adrenaline rush in your body starts to produce nausea. The extreme highs and lows of the ride create panic because the ride is totally out of your control.

We begin recovery when we admit that our lives feel like one big roller-coaster ride. The addictions that at one time seemed exciting no longer ease our pain. In fact, they now cause serious problems. The only way to stop the ride is to admit that our lives have become unmanageable. Accepting our powerlessness lays the foundation on which we build our recovery.

If we do not practice Step One on a consistent basis, we are destined
to repeat our addictions again.

                                                        CSH

Give ear to my words, O LORD
Consider my meditation.
Give heed to the voice of my cry,
My King and my God,
For to You I will pray.
                    —PS. 5:1–2

I once read a story about a mother who had two sons to raise alone on what she could bring in by babysitting. The younger, a six year old, was struck by a car and had suffered a severe concussion and broken right thigh bone.

This woman knew she did not have the power to solve her problems alone, so she prayed that God would give others the willingness to help. Her story appeared in the newspaper and she received over $20,000 in gifts, plus cards and letters from people showing they cared.

Sitting in her son's hospital room, this mother gave the glory to God. She said, "I knew the Lord would help. I just thank God for moving in the hearts of so many people. I pray for the same blessing for those people in the future."

Believing in a power greater than yourself can become just as natural to you as it was to that woman, and his miracles can be just as great.

_____

Miracles happen to those who expect them.

                                        BLB

> *"Do not be afraid of their faces,*
> *For I am with you to deliver you."*
> —JER. 1:8

Many of God's servants felt an overwhelming sense of inadequacy when faced with a new challenge. We read in the Old Testament of a young man named Jeremiah who was called by God to deliver a message to the people of Judah. Jeremiah refused at first because he felt afraid and inadequate, but God promised that he would provide the power to complete the task.

Admitting our powerlessness often confuses us, since we felt out of control all along. Admitting powerlessness in the program means that we give up on willpower, strength, and rationalizing because they didn't work. It means giving up efforts to do it on our own.

God waits for you to give up on all of your futile efforts, so that you realize your desperate need for him. While facing this monumental change, you may relate to the fear of Jeremiah, but take courage in accepting that God's power is often demonstrated in our inadequacy.

—————————

God, help me to accept my weakness so that I can trust in your strength.

CSH

> *"I will pray the Father, and He will give you*
> *another Helper, that He may abide with you*
> *forever . . . but you know Him, for He dwells*
> *with you and will be in you."*
>
> —JOHN 14:16–17

There are many reasons for loneliness: death of a loved one, being a senior citizen tucked away in a retirement center, betrayal by a friend causing us to isolate ourselves rather than risk trusting someone. The most profound loneliness is the sense of separation from God.

Today we have the ability to put someone on the moon, but with all our intelligence, we cannot put someone else back in communion with God. This is a job that we can only do for ourselves.

When Joshua became Moses' successor as leader of Israel, God assured him with the words, "I will be with you" (Josh. 1:5). Jesus told his disciples, "I am with you always, even to the end of the age" (Matt. 28:20).

As we sit in our loneliness there are many others feeling the same way. We can overcome our feelings of isolation by reaching out to others and by accepting the presence of Christ who is with us always.

When we feel separated from God, it is because we have moved away, not him.

BLB

> *"Fear not, for I have redeemed you;*
> *I have called you by your name;*
> *You are Mine."*
> —ISA. 43:1

Alcoholism is a generational family disease. As one struggles with the addiction, the disease overtakes the whole family and can pass on to succeeding generations. George struggled with alcoholism for twenty-five years. His legacy to his sons was alcoholism. In the mind of the alcoholic there is fear, anger, and insecurity: fear of being out of control, anger at everyone who is trying to control the situation, and insecurity due to the unpredictable nature of the disease.

If you are recovering from alcoholism, you must make amends with family members. You must not only ask for forgiveness for past behavior, but also demonstrate new behavior. Replace fear with confidence in the Lord. Replace anger with love, kindness, and consideration. Replace insecurity with knowledge that only by the power of God can the miracle of recovery take place. Only in this way can you relieve yourself of the guilt over past behavior.

To those of you who have the problem of the family disease, there is hope, for God loves you and is with you in your struggle.

———————

Everyone deserves the dignity of living their own life, but when we struggle, God wants us to know he is there with us.

BLB

> *"Consecrate yourselves today to the LORD, that He may bestow on you a blessing."*   —EX. 32:29

Letting go can often be difficult. One woman just beginning recovery came to group after drinking heavily. She was so afraid of her feelings that she wanted to anesthetize them.

Her relapse made me think of the doves that perch outside my window on a large power line, which carries a heavy current of electricity. The birds suffer no harm when they contact the wire, because they touch nothing else. But, if I could lean far enough out my window to grasp the wire, death would come to me like a swift lightening bolt, because the outside walls would act as a ground. My body would be a channel through which the current would flow in damaging power.

We are in danger if we reach one hand out to God and still hold onto our addiction. Yet, if we reach out to him with both hands, realizing we are powerless to control our lives, he will give us strength and its blessings.

_____

God is patiently waiting for us to reach out to him. Only he can provide the strength we need for the journey of recovery.

CSH

> *I am weary with my groaning;*
> *All night I make my bed swim;*
> *I drench my couch with my tears.*
> —PS. 6:6

Some nights we toss and turn, trying to solve one problem after another. We think if we had just said something or done something, things would be different. As hard as we work at the problem, we usually don't come up with a solution.

In the Bible, David suffered from some of the same feelings. He had been attracted to a married woman. He wanted her for himself, so he took her. Then, compounding the sin of adultery, he sent the woman's husband to the front lines of battle to be killed. David's sinful nature caused him much unrest, much tossing and turning and groaning in the night. Eventually, though, he turned to God and cried out for his forgiveness. David shows us in his psalms how to cry out to our Lord.

———————

When morning gilds the skies, my heart awaking cries, may Jesus Christ be praised (Anonymous, German, Nineteenth Century).

BLB

In the LORD I put my trust.
—PS. 11:1

We feel powerless because we cannot change another person. Only God has the power to change people. So when we feel powerless, we need to focus on the Lord.

"The LORD is in His holy temple" (Ps. 11:4). God is on his throne. He rules the world and the affairs of human beings. Our president is not our ultimate ruler; no world power is going to solve the problems of the world. God has a plan.

"His eyelids test the sons of men" (Ps. 11:4). God is involved in the lives of his people. He heals deep wounds of the soul. He restores broken relationships; he opens hearts to love.

Gloria, struggling with recovery, found peace in the above psalms. She found that she did not have the power to change another or the power to control the world. She found, through the grace of our Lord, the peace and serenity that she needed.

God holds the whole world in his hands.

BLB

Have mercy on me, O Lord, for I am weak;
O Lord, heal me, for my bones are troubled.
                                        —PS. 6:2

Cynthia told me during our session that many times she felt like she was being pushed in one direction and pulled in another. She would be involved in a task and someone would interrupt her; or she would be interrupted during visits with friends or at work by the telephone. She also related how her sleep was interrupted by the children. The interruptions were causing her to feel stressed and she was having a hard time in her recovery because of them.

We all have these interruptions. How do we deal with them? Do we get tight-lipped or do we smile? Do we order the other person to go away or do we welcome the interruption? However we handle them, our recovery comes first.

My mother-in-law was a beautiful example of someone who very graciously accepts interruptions in her life. She celebrated her eightieth birthday last winter. During the years I knew her, she taught me to accept what cannot be changed. Learning to deal with stress caused by others pushing and pulling on us is part of our recovery program.

God, grant me the serenity to accept the things I cannot change (The Serenity Prayer).

                                        BLB

*"And I will pray the Father, and He will give you
another Helper, that He may abide with you
forever."*   —JOHN 14:16

John is a recovering alcoholic. Not only does he regularly attend AA meetings, but he reaches out to other alcoholics who need help. One night he received a call at midnight from a man who was out of work. He had really hit bottom and wanted help. John went to his house and sat with him all night, talking with him about how someone had come along at his lowest point and had helped him turn his life around. John shared the Twelve-Step program of AA with this man and then went with him to an AA meeting. This is the way recovering alcoholics stay sober—by comforting others and helping them get sober.

We can give comfort to those in need in three ways. First, we must work the Twelve-Step program for ourselves. Second, we must be concerned about other people's problems and try to help them spiritually. And finally, we should remember not to talk about our problems all the time; we should instead offer the wisdom of the Twelve Steps.

Life holds many surprises for us each day, but meditating on God's Word and working the Twelve Steps will lead you toward health and happiness.

BLB

*We came to believe that a Power greater than
ourselves could restore us to sanity.*

When we are consumed by addiction, we have given
our heart, soul, and mind to a false god. That addiction
may be to drugs, alcohol, work, or food. This is the
same as codependency. A codependent reaches out
externally for something or someone or uses a behavior to gain comfort for internal pain.

To comfort ourselves in a healthy way, we reach inside ourselves. If we have not taken the Spirit of the
Lord into our heart, soul, and mind, then when we
reach inside ourselves, we'll come up empty-handed.

Feed your body, soul, and mind with your Twelve
Step recovery material, your daily devotional material
and your sponsor's, counselor's, or minister's guidance.
Spend time daily in meditation with the Lord. Speak to
him in prayer, but also spend time in meditation, listening for his words to you. Attend Twelve Step meetings,
to gain support from others who share their experiences in overcoming addictions.

---

*Put your relationship with God first and the rest will open to your
understanding.*

                                                    BLB

> *Trust in the LORD with all your heart,*
> *And lean not on your own understanding;*
> *In all your ways acknowledge Him,*
> *And He shall direct your paths.*
> —PROV. 3:5–6

Around the country of Greenland, countless icebergs float in the frigid waters. These icebergs come in all shapes and sizes, from the very small to the massive ones that reach skyward. The movement of these icebergs intrigues people because the small ones move in a different direction from the large ones. These opposite movements occur because surface winds are able to move the tiny ones, but the huge masses of ice are only moved by deep ocean currents.

In our own lives, the gusts of wind we face may be the unpredictable changes we encounter throughout recovery. These changes often feel overwhelming. We draw encouragement from knowing that even when the winds of change threaten us on the surface, God has everything under control. God's will for our lives and his unchanging love for us form the unseen current that leads us in a healthy direction.

The more we practice placing our trust in God, the less we struggle with the surface winds. He promises to direct our paths with his love and power.

I will trust that God plans to guide me toward a healthy recovery.
CSH

For the message of the cross is foolishness to those who are perishing, but to us who are being saved it is the power of God.   —1 COR. 1:18

There is a story about a man who built his house near a river that would rise during a rainstorm. He had been warned that if the river rose, his home would flood. He replied, "The Lord will provide." One day the rains came, the river rose, and his home was flooded. A rowboat came by and offered to carry him to dry land. He replied, "The Lord will provide." Later he climbed on the roof of his house. A motorboat passed by and its boatman offered him help. He replied, "The Lord will provide." As the waters rose higher, he climbed atop the chimney. The pilot of a helicopter circling overhead called down to him and offered to lift him off the roof. He replied, "The Lord will provide."

After drowning, he arrived in heaven. The Lord asked him what he was doing there. The man replied, "Waiting, Lord, for you to provide." The Lord replied, "What more did you want? I sent a rowboat, a motorboat, and a helicopter."

When we ask the Lord to show us the way, he gives us a map to follow. The Twelve Steps are a map to a healthy way of life.

                                                    BLB

We each have so much control over our own
feelings that we are able to choose not to give
control of ourselves to others.
                              —DONNA TILLINGHAST

People often complain that their week starts out just fine, but then someone says or does something to make them angry or to hurt their feelings. The week seems to go downhill from there, they say. I usually stop them at that point and ask for a "truth check."

When we say that other people "make" us have a certain feeling, we are actually saying that we have no choice in how we respond. The truth is that, in most situations, you have the freedom to decide how you will respond. It's like taking a multiple choice test. For example, if someone tells you that your new outfit looks terrible, you have several choices. You can: (a) get angry and make a hurtful remark in return, (b) allow your feelings to be hurt and choose never to wear the outfit again, (c) realize that their comment really says something about them, not you. Choosing A or B would lead you to blame the other person for your feelings. The healthy choice, C, would remind you that what really matters is that you like your new outfit.

Choices give us the freedom to control our own feelings and
responses.

                                                          CSH

*But the fruit of the Spirit is love, joy, peace,
longsuffering, kindness, goodness, faithfulness,
gentleness, self-control. Against such there is
no law.*
                                        —GAL. 5:22–23

God's plan is for us to live in love and peace with everyone. I think God gives us children to help us learn something about that plan.

One day a father was rushing his son to get dressed for Sunday school. A dozen times he told him to hurry, but his son kept dawdling. The father was becoming impatient with his son. Finally, father and son got in the car and headed for church. Again the father issued orders to hurry. As they crossed the parking lot, the father turned one more time to hurry his son along, and what he saw stopped him. There was his son, only four, on a beautiful sunny Sunday morning, leaning over a flowerbed with his face buried in the bloom of a beautiful rose. All thought of hurrying was lost. The father learned the lesson of patience. His son had taught him the beauty of rejoicing in the day the Lord had made.

God teaches us love, joy, peace, longsuffering, kindness, goodness, faithfulness, gentleness, and self-control through the actions of others.

BLB

Insanity means doing the same thing over and over, expecting different results.   —ANONYMOUS

An alcoholic drinks to try to make his problems disappear. A husband or wife enters into an affair, believing somehow it will change a situation at home. A man works eighty hours a week trying to change something from his past. In each case, the results remain the same. The alcoholic ends up alone, his problems still intact. The husband or wife comes home ashamed and afraid of being found out. The man working too hard never changes the hurts of his past. They each think, though, *maybe next time it will work.*

The addict, no matter what the addiction, sinks deeper and deeper. Well-meaning people offer excellent advice and help, but sadly, the warnings go unheeded.

Then one day an unexpected event happens that forces the addict to face reality head-on. The alcoholic drives under the influence and hits a bus, killing innocent children. The illicit affair is exposed. The workaholic gets laid off. At that moment, they cry out to God, the only one capable of restoring sanity to a shattered life. For all three, the pathway to God was painful and had some chilling consequences, but they finally found the Power greater than themselves.

In Step Two we learn to stop our crazy behavior. Our sanity has been restored.

CSH

So they said, "Believe on the Lord Jesus Christ, and
you will be saved, you and your household."
                                        —ACTS 16:31

Holidays are difficult times for families who live with alcoholism. Alcoholics are so predictably unpredictable. We know they will get drunk and ruin everything, but we just don't know when and where. For weeks before the family gathering, we begin thinking of ways we can make things different this year. How can we keep the alcoholic from getting drunk? We sometimes wish the holidays wouldn't even come.

During this time we get more and more anxious. The anxiety drains us emotionally. We get irritable, fatigue sets in, and often we get sick. If we grew up in an alcoholic home, many of us resort to drinking alcohol in order to deal with the pain of these family gatherings. We have taken on the burden of controlling another person. It is insane to live this way.

We must remember that we have choices. We can turn our feelings of powerlessness over to God. We can live with Christ today or we can die with alcoholism every day.

———————————

"Therefore do not worry about tomorrow, for tomorrow will worry about its own things" (Matt. 6:34).

                                        BLB

I shall light a candle of understanding in thine heart which shall not be put out.
—APOCRYPHA

A dictionary defines *insanity* as "great folly; extreme senselessness, an inability to manage one's own affairs." If we look at insanity from this perspective, we see that much of our behavior was insane. We blamed other people and things for our addictions instead of accepting responsibility for our own actions.

As we begin to rely on God as our Higher Power, he brings us to an awareness of how our dependencies deceived and disabled us. As we attempted to control our addictions by ourselves, we searched for outside causes for our disability. Believing that we could control our obsessions, compulsions, depression, and anxiety on our own was insane. We now see that we need God's help in order to become healthy.

God helps us get a clear picture of our situation when we spend time with other people who have had similar experiences. We must work the program one day at a time. Our quality of life improves as we become more dependent on our Higher Power.

As I begin to understand my problems, I can trust God for solutions.
CSH

*For the good that I will to do, I do not do; but the
evil I will not to do, that I practice.*

—ROM. 7:19

We all have basic needs. The most important are for
food, safety, and shelter. Once we are fed and protected, then we seek love. Love is a strong drive and
also a basic need for survival. God saw this need in
Adam, so he created Eve. Adam had food, safety, and
shelter in the garden, but he needed another person to
relate to. When we have these needs met, then we
grow with others. Without these needs being met, we
feel empty and powerless.

Jesus had the same needs we do as a human being.
He needed food, shelter, safety, and love. He showed
us how God loved him and provided for him. He
showed us his need for rest when he pulled away from
others to a quiet place. He showed us how God wanted
us to love our brothers and sisters by loving the people
around him. He showed us his need to depend on God
and for relationship with God when he prayed.

This is how we grow also, by being sheltered, nourished, and protected, and by developing a relationship
with God.

---

*Only by a power greater than ourselves can we achieve what is
God's will.*

BLB

*"For I know the thoughts that I think toward you,
says the LORD, thoughts of peace and not of evil,
to give you a future and a hope."*

—JER. 29:11

Many people wear glasses or contact lenses to correct their vision. Nearsightedness, or myopia, means that a person is unable to bring distant objects into focus.

Many of us struggle with spiritual myopia. We only focus on immediate events. We fear looking out into the distance at our future. Instead we create a nearsighted comfort zone, which only includes what we know we can do for ourselves.

Visual myopia can be corrected by using the proper lens. Correction of spiritual myopia involves three steps. First, we find confidence knowing that God is present in our lives and that he understands every need we have.

Second, we rest in the promises of God. He promises to never leave us or forsake us. However, many of us have a difficult time trusting these promises, because our parents did not always keep their promises. We must remember that God has never backed out on a single promise.

Last, we draw confidence from God's power and trust in his faithfulness.

We can look toward to the future, see things we cannot do in our own strength, and trust God to guide us.

CSH

> *God, grant me the serenity to accept the things I*
> *cannot change. . . .*   —REINHOLD NIEBUHR

Serenity is a state of mind where your thoughts are not running in thousands of directions at one time, or where your mind is not so vacant and confused that there is nothing rational coming out. Serenity is a state of feeling whole and at peace and thinking clearly.

We pray what is called "The Serenity Prayer" by Reinhold Niebuhr, and we ask God for serenity. How do we know when he answers our prayers? How do we know when we are serene? Do we have to be serene before we can accept things? Or do we have to accept certain things to be serene? What is this acceptance business?

Let's look at the other side of this question. If we can become serene enough, we can accept without trying to change others. If we can become serene enough, we can tend to our own business and let others take care of themselves. If we are serene enough, we have love, patience, kindness, gentleness, joy, peace, and self-control.

What a reason to pray for serenity!

BLB

Whenever I am afraid,
I will trust in you.
—PS. 56:3

Every New Year's Day many of us create long lists of resolutions. We vow to let go of old thoughts, feelings, and behaviors, and we try to replace them with positive changes. It doesn't take us long to return to our old habits. We make excuses and put off changing until later.

One of the pluses of recovery is that we no longer rely on our own strength to change. We ask for help and receive it. We find the freedom to start over at any time. Once we decide to humbly admit to our powerlessness over an impulse or substance, then we are free to begin a new life.

In Psalm 56:3, we are told that when we are afraid we can trust in God. The new changes may be scary at times, but God's power leads us to a place of restored sanity. We can cling to him like a frightened child holds onto a parent. God always supports us, and his love never fails.

_____

My fears seem to lose their power when I share them with God and with others.

CSH

"If you abide in My word, you are My disciples indeed. And you shall know the truth, and the truth shall make you free."   —JOHN 8:31–32

When I was sixteen, I committed my life to serving the Lord in some way. I thought I wanted to be a missionary. A few years later, I fell in love and married.

In later years, as I struggled through the teenage years of my three children, I thought back over my commitment to be a missionary. I thought the Lord had deserted me by not providing me the opportunity to serve him as a missionary.

Little did I know at that time when we give ourselves and our lives to the Lord, he puts us through the fire, like a steelworker does, to make fine steel. Then he tempers us to work on removing the imperfections. The job would go much faster if we didn't work so hard at hanging onto them. Then he tests our strength by giving us problems to deal with to help us develop patience and self-control.

Today I am able to serve him, not as a missionary, but as a wife, mother, grandmother, counselor, and friend. He is using me where I am.

God is training us to do his work. He just wants it done in his way and in his time.

BLB

*"For the eyes of the LORD run to and fro
throughout the whole earth, to show Himself
strong on behalf of those whose heart is loyal
to Him."*   —2 CHRON. 16:9a

When children say their prayers before bed each night, they comprehend God as a heavenly version of their earthly father. Some of us had fathers who physically or emotionally abandoned us or who were abusive due to their own addictions. We grew up assuming that God the Father is like our earthly father. If our earthly father rejected us, we think our heavenly Father will too. We often feel that no matter how hard we try, we can't get close to God.

Each of us has a deep longing to be close to someone. In the verse for today, God tells us that he is looking for people who desire to know him. He longs to be close to us. We may have felt that acceptance by our fathers could be earned through performance or good behavior, but God accepts us right where we are, no matter what we have done. His love for us has no conditions and no strings attached.

As we yield our will and lives to him, God "shows himself strong" on our behalf. He is ready and willing to provide the strength we need for recovery.

CSH

> *"But the Helper, the Holy Spirit, whom the Father*
> *will send in My name, He will teach you all things,*
> *and bring to your remembrance all things that I*
> *said to you."*   —JOHN 14:26

We sometimes feel all alone in our fear. We fear lone-liness, abandonment, and rejection. Because of our need to protect ourselves and survive as a child, we developed defenses. Our defenses can be to isolate ourselves, to avoid talking about how we feel, and to believe that we can't trust anyone.

On the last night of his life, Jesus went to the garden to pray and asked his friends to go with him. He didn't want to be alone in his fear. He even told Peter, James and John, "My soul is exceedingly sorrowful, even to death. Stay here and watch with Me" (Matt. 26:38). When he returned from his prayers, they were asleep. He said, "What, could you not watch with Me one hour?" Even Jesus' friends let him down. So Jesus pro-vided that when we felt alone, he would watch and wait with us.

This is promised to us in Step Two. God is the power that stays with us through all pain and heals us.

No man has ever been where God is not.

                                            BLB

"And the rain descended, the floods came, and the winds blew and beat on that house; and it did not fall, for it was founded on the rock."

—MATT. 7:25

Jesus told a story of two men who built houses in different locations. One man foolishly built his house on sand. When the storm came and the wind and rain beat upon the house, it fell. The second man wisely built the foundation of his house on solid rock. The floods came and the winds blew, but the house did not fall, because it was set on the rock.

In our addictions we have been like the foolish man. Our own wisdom and ingenuity never brought us the results we hoped for. We looked to ourselves for solutions and were unable to solve life's problems. For many of us who built our house on sand, the realization of our own powerlessness came slowly. Often after a storm of destruction, we sought to rebuild in exactly the same spot. We repeated the patterns of our addictive behavior over and over again.

Sanity can be restored as we realize the futility of our efforts for control. Seeking God's wisdom and guidance, we can begin to rebuild our lives on a solid foundation that will stand through the storms of life.

I will consciously surrender my will to God's will so that he can begin to rebuild my life.

CSH

> *"I am the light of the world. He who follows Me shall not walk in darkness, but have the light of life."*
> —JOHN 8:12

The pressures we face today create stress in our daily living. How we handle that stress is based on how we think and act. We may lash out at people or events, we may just want to run away from our problems, or we may comfort ourselves in an unhealthy way by using drugs or alcohol. We learned the behavior we use to handle stress from our parents. They may have blamed someone else for their problems, they may have rationalized the reasons for their reaction to stress, they may have covered up their feelings with busy work, or they may have just denied their feelings.

When we are under stress we need to talk to someone about how we feel and what we think. Good communication with others can help us express our frustrations and fears and feel support and hope. We also need to call on God for guidance, strength, and wisdom through meditation and prayer.

"Because a thing seems difficult for you, do not think it is impossible for anyone to accomplish. But whatever is possible for another, believe that you, too, are capable of it" (Marcus Aurelius).

BLB

> *You number my wanderings;*
> *Put my tears into Your bottle;*
> *Are they not in Your book?*
> —PS. 56:8

Many therapists believe that abuse victims stop growing emotionally at whatever age their abuse began. They physically grew into adults, but the inner child is emotionally stunted. Many hurting people are stuck in vicious cycles of pain, addiction, guilt, shame, and more pain. These adults have great difficulty nurturing their emotional child in healthy ways.

Many of us had parents who severely damaged us emotionally. We can find hope in Psalm 27:10, where we are offered these encouraging words: "When my father and my mother forsake me, then the LORD will take care of me." God knows and feels our pain. In Psalm 34:18 he promises us, "The LORD is near to those who have a broken heart, and saves such as have a contrite spirit."

The most gracious thing we can do for our inner child is to take him or her to our loving heavenly Father for emotional healing. One of the many names for God in the Bible is Jehovah Rapha, which means "the God who heals." We can trust in God, who is able to lead us down the road of recovery and healing.

Since our addictions failed to solve our problems, why not turn to the one who has the power and desire to deliver us from our self-destructive ways?

CSH

For it is God who works in you both to will and to
do for His good pleasure.   —PHIL. 2:13

Being offered the opportunity to do God's work is overwhelming at times. But even before we were born, God had a plan for our life. As we struggle with his will, we become aware of a sense of insanity about our way of living and thinking. As we turn our life and thoughts over to him, we begin to see a way out of this insanity.

When we try to create our own tasks and thoughts, we fail to reach the hearts of those the Lord has sent us to serve. When we try to write on our own power, our mind goes blank. When we try to create artistically, God makes a sunset far more beautiful. When we try to meet our own deadlines, time runs out. We need to remind ourselves that God will reach the hearts of other people. He will change the behavior of people who have gotten out of his will.

God has created the opportunity for each of us to serve him in a special way. He makes the way possible and then he gives us the power to do the task. May we learn to give God the opportunity to speak through us.

Lord, fill my mouth with worthwhile stuff, and shut it when I have said enough.

BLB

First of all, we had to quit playing God. It didn't work.
—*BIG BOOK* OF *ALCOHOLICS ANONYMOUS*

Children often learn geometric shapes by playing with a toy containing openings in the form of a circle, triangle, square, and rectangle. The object is to place the matching piece through each hole.

Young children become frustrated at times when they try to place a square piece through a round opening. Instead of trying a different piece, they may continue to hit the toy and try to force in the mismatched piece.

God created us with a God-shaped vacuum so that we would feel a need to have a personal relationship with him. We often misunderstand this longing within.

Just as a child repeatedly tries to force the wrong piece to fit, we often seek to fill our internal void with people or substances that are not sufficient to meet our needs. Repeating this pattern sends us into the addictions that make us feel insane.

Only a personal spiritual relationship with God satisfies the deepest needs and longings of our heart. When we invite God to fill the void in us, his presence creates the perfect fit.

———————

God is waiting to fill your emptiness with his love and power.

CSH

"For with God nothing will be impossible."
—LUKE 1:37

How many times a day do I worship false gods, putting something or someone before God? Some things that come to mind are money, food, or a new car. My loved ones can also become too important.

Many of us are addicted to these things. Compulsive shoppers and gamblers put their addiction first in their life. Food can become a more comforting factor to someone than the power of God through meditation. Submission to an abusive parent or spouse can distort one's perception of God as the loving, caring Father.

God tells us to put him first and all else will follow in his way. This is a very hard concept to understand in a practical way, but one day a clear picture came to mind.

If I concentrate solely on pleasing God, then I will become what God wants me to be. That person then will be to others a reflection of God's love. By putting God first, all relationships, all addictions, and all compulsive behavior will fade, because we cannot serve two masters at the same time.

If we serve people, we will only become like them, but if we serve God, we will rise to greater heights than ever imagined.

BLB

There is nothing either good nor bad but thinking makes it so.   —WILLIAM SHAKESPEARE

Craig came into therapy at age nineteen, feeling overwhelmed by the stresses of his freshman year. It became clear that his family system was very rigid. Craig felt he had never met his father's expectations, and therefore he had very low self-esteem.

He worried about getting into a fraternity, as his parents expected him to. No matter how many things went right at a fraternity social, he focused on the one thing that went wrong. Once he forgot a fellow's name, and another time, he tripped while walking through a door. He magnified the one small thing he considered a failure to the exclusion of everything else.

Many of us have this problem of not being able to see the forest for the trees. We focus on what is wrong with us instead of looking at what is right. No wonder our self-esteem feels so fragile and defeated! It's hard to like ourselves when all we see is the negative.

Most of our daily activity is neither right nor wrong. Forgetting someone's name or tripping on a rug is not wrong. It is human. Accepting our humanity brings us to realize our need for a Higher Power to restore us to a place of truthful thinking.

We need to look at the whole forest instead of focusing on just one tree.

CSH

Jesus said to him, "If you can believe, all things are possible to him who believes." —MARK 9:23

Have you ever watched toddlers learning how to walk? They take a step or two and then fall down hard on their bottoms. They sometimes cry and sometimes laugh, but they always get back up and try again.

Why is it that the older we get, when we fall down hard, we tend to stay down longer and even sit there feeling sorry for ourselves?

Oh, to have the faith of that toddler, to just take one step at a time, and when we fall, to get back up and try again and again.

God offers us that faith—faith that can perform miracles, faith that when we are down, we can reach up to him, and he will give us the strength to try again. All we have to do is believe in him. He tells us that faith will move mountains.

Lois struggled hard trying to push Jerry into treatment. Jerry was rooted as firmly as a mountain, but when Lois let go and let God work in Jerry's life, the mountain was moved. The miracle of Jerry's recovery could not have happened without faith in God's ability.

The grace of God allows us to pick ourselves up, dust ourselves off, and start all over again.

BLB

*When we surrendered to our Higher Power, the
journey began.*   —ANONYMOUS

Mr. Scott brought his son, Ken, to counseling, because after an angry outburst, he ran away from home.
Further exploration revealed that Mr. Scott grew up in
an alcoholic family system filled with physical vio-
lence. He used his workaholism to escape from the
pain of his childhood.

Ken acted out all of the unexpressed pain and anger
as the scapegoat of the family. His acting out took the
attention off Dad's workaholism and gave the family a
reason to stay together.

The Bible clearly states that patterns of dysfunction
are passed on in families for generations. Even though
Mr. Scott wanted a different lifestyle for his son, he
passed on the dysfunction in the same way he received
it.

Only God and his power can show us how to make
"the buck stop here." With God's help, the dysfunctional patterns of the past can be changed and recovery can begin.

*I will search for dysfunctional patterns so that the chains of the past
can be broken.*

CSH

But God, who is rich in mercy, because of His great love with which He loved us, even when we were dead in trespasses, made us alive together with Christ.

—EPH. 2:4–5

Sometimes we feel all alone, deserted, abandoned. What can we do? We feel so powerless over our lives. We have nothing to get up for. No one needs us or wants us. We sink into self-pity.

When Jesus was on the cross, he cried out to his Father, "Why have you forsaken me?" He had spent his whole life serving others and now, when he was in greatest need, he felt alone. But in the moments of Jesus' aloneness, he had a choice. He reached out for God, and when he did he was no longer alone.

We have the same choice. In our aloneness, we can reach out to God. When we do we will no longer feel alone.

———————

When we reach out and give ourselves to God, he gives us the peace and serenity that lets us know we are not alone.

BLB

*And God said to Moses, "I AM WHO I AM." And He
said, "Thus you shall say to the children of Israel, 'I
AM has sent me to you.'"*
                                                —EX. 3:14

When God called Moses to lead the children of Israel
out of slavery in Egypt, Moses had several questions.
He asked God who he should say had sent him as the
leader. God responded that Moses should tell the people that "I AM" had sent him.

When we are discouraged, we can remember that
God is still the great "I AM." We can fill in the blank of
what we need for God to be for us. "I AM" your com-
forter, encourager, strength, friend, confidant, healer,
guide, heavenly Father, or support. God has the awesome ability to be what we need, when we need it. He
shows concern for all of our feelings and knows us intimately.

God is perfect, and his abilities are limitless and
multifaceted. People have let us down in the past, but
God remains trustworthy and will never fail us. We can
place our confidence in his ability and desire to take
care of us.

———————

I will trust in God to provide for each of my needs.

CSH

So then neither he who plants is anything, nor he
who waters, but God who gives the increase.
— 1 COR. 3:7

Every spring we like to plant a vegetable garden. It is fun choosing which seeds we'll plant each year.

We diligently prepare the soil, then we make a furrow, plant the seeds, and gently cover them with dirt. We nourish them with water, and we make sure to plant them in the sun. Then we label the rows, so we will know what is planted. We have done all we can for the moment. So we rest and wait to see the first shoots come out of the ground. As the shoots emerge, we water and feed our garden. When our garden is fruitful we rejoice at what a good job we have done. We feel such a sense of power over what we have created.

But did we create this abundance of new life? Who provided the sun for warmth? Who provided the water for nourishment? Who looked over this garden night and day, while we tended to our earthly duties?

We can work hand in hand with God to carry out a task, but when we turn the final product over to him, we can rejoice in his power.

BLB

> *No man is an island unto himself.*
> —ANONYMOUS

Jill sat in my office and wept. She told me she had been a cocaine addict, but had stopped using two years ago. In recent months she experienced panic attacks. She described her temper as "always ready to explode." She sought therapy mainly because she feared her panic attacks and angry outbursts would destroy her marriage.

Jill had tried to stop her addiction cold turkey. Although she prays and reads her Bible each day, she feels frustrated and let down by God because of her recurring panic and flaring temper.

Jill's case proves that no amount of logic, rationalizing, or spiritualizing will stop our addictions. We may stop one behavior, but the root issues begin to show up in other areas of our lives, such as panic and anger. We often replace one addiction with another until we deal with the real problems.

We all need help in working through our recovery process. None of us can make it alone. The healing of Twelve-Step programs comes through the support and encouragement we receive from and give in return to the members of our group.

I choose to reach out and allow others to help me in my recovery.
CSH

We made a decision to turn our will and our lives over to the care of God as we understand him.

The Twelve-Step program of Alcoholics Anonymous is a way of healing for alcoholics. Programs are also provided for their families. Alcoholics need support during recovery and the best way for families to give them that support is to be involved in appropriate programs themselves, because the whole family is affected by alcoholism.

Norman Vincent Peale wrote that the Twelve Steps are a way of life. When we look at them, this is true. We admit we are powerless over alcohol and others. We accept that only God can return us to sanity. Then comes the hard part. We have to make a decision to turn our will over to God.

We sometimes respond, "Oh, I can do that if he'll just let me tell him how I want it done." God is all powerful and full of wisdom. His plans transcend generations. He created the heavens and the earth. Why should I want to tell God how to do his job?

Lord, help me to let go and leave things in your hands.

BLB

The best way to eat an elephant is one bite at a time.   —ANONYMOUS

Most things are handled more easily in bite-sized pieces. When faced with a major task, divide the task into smaller sections, and take each piece one at a time. This holds true whether planning a wedding, packing to move, or directing a project at work.

The same idea holds true for our prayer life. Many of us are just learning to pray, and our requests may at times seem huge and world-encompassing. Frustration increases when we feel as though we're praying without results.

We see more answered prayer when we break our requests down to bite-size. Make specific requests that you believe are according to God's will. For example, instead of asking God to help you forgive all the people who have hurt you, try working on praying for the restoration of one specific relationship through forgiveness. Start by making bite-sized requests. They're not overwhelming and are much easier to swallow.

Today I will ask God for something specific.

CSH

For by grace you have been saved through faith,
and that not of yourselves; it is the gift of God.
                                              —EPH. 2:8

When we hear the word *denial* we seem to think that it only describes people who refuse to admit that they have an addiction problem. Denial applies to all of us who make excuses, blame others, rationalize, try to fix others, or enable others not to deal with their own problems. Denial prevents us from facing ourselves and provides us with a false sense of self-esteem. Denial keeps us from taking responsibility for our thoughts, feelings, and actions.

Think about our thoughts. How many times have we thought, "If so and so would just change, then I would be all right"? How many times have we refused to accept responsibility for our feelings? We do this by repressing our anger and clamming up or by raging and spewing out our anger on those around us. This is controlling others, rather than openly communicating our thoughts and feelings. We stay in denial to protect ourselves. Denial is what keeps the addiction process going.

_____

We cannot solve others' problems, but we can show them how to solve problems by accepting responsibility for solving our own.

                                                        BLB

*"Then you will call upon Me and go and pray to
Me, and I will listen to you. And you will seek Me
and find Me, when you search for Me with all
your heart."*   —JER. 29:12–13

 We feel skeptical when people give us their word on
something. Maybe our parents made promises that
they did not always keep. Some of us experienced relationships where a partner promised never to leave us,
and we felt crushed and abandoned by their departure
from our lives. We experienced pain and disappointment from the broken promises of people we cared for.
Repeated hurt convinced us not to trust anymore.

 The pain of this type of thinking often drives our
addictions. Our addictions promised relief from our
pain, but they eventually led us into more suffering.

 When we come to Step Three, we examine our
thinking patterns. We decide to give God control of our
lives, but do we trust him to take care of us? We often
question God and his promises due to our past experience with broken pledges. We need to remember,
though, that God is trustworthy. He desires to produce
healing in our wounded hearts, and he has never broken a single promise. God tells us we can call to him,
and he will answer us. When we seek him, we will find
him.

I place my confidence in the promises of God.

CSH

Cause me to hear Your lovingkindness
in the morning,
For in You do I trust;
Cause me to know the way in which
I should walk,
For I lift up my soul to You.

—PS. 143:8

When denial is at work in our life, it is like being in a room with the shutters closed. No light can come in. We are alone in the darkness.

This denial acts as a defense against what may be on the other side—loneliness, pain, anger, responsibility, or love. If we keep the defenses up, we won't have to face it.

In Step Three, we begin slowly opening the shutters. We admit we may have a problem. Then we admit we don't have any control over the problem. After that we open the shutters a little wider and realize that we don't have control over anything or anybody.

The light is coming through the shutters in little rays. One beam falls on our relationships with others; another beam falls on our work routine. As the light gets brighter, more rays shine on the unhealthy ways we are behaving. Our attitudes and thoughts begin to be exposed. We realize that we are insane to be living like this.

The light shining in our darkness is God's love shining through to us.
BLB

> *"For I know the thoughts that I think toward you,*
> *says the LORD, thoughts of peace and not of evil,*
> *to give you a future and a hope."*
>   —JER. 29:11

In Step Three, we realize that God is our Higher Power, and we allow him to control our will and care for our needs. Jeremiah lets us know that we are very special to God. As a matter of fact, God is thinking thoughts of peace and not of evil toward us. Evil has pulled us into our painful addictions, but God is planning to produce a peaceful place of healing in our lives.

Many of us wondered about our future. Before recovery, looking forward seemed desolate, painful, and hopeless. Those feelings dwelt in our hearts because our dependencies raged out of control. Now that we have turned our will and lives over to God, he has plans for our future. We find hope in what lies ahead for us, because God is leading us to a spiritual awakening. Our hope can be renewed by the knowledge that God can now assume control of every area of our lives.

I will be hopeful knowing that I can look forward to the future.
                                                              CSH

Likewise the Spirit also helps in our weaknesses.
For we do not know what we should pray for as
we ought, but the Spirit Himself makes intercession
for us with groanings which cannot be uttered.
—ROM. 8:26

One of the things that I lost during my obsession with changing another person was my sense of humor. I allowed my thoughts and actions to be influenced by what others did and said while they were struggling with their own illnesses. Nothing seemed to have a bright side. Nothing seemed fun or funny anymore. I felt like a real sourpuss.

I began to pray for guidance to make it through the next hour without becoming obsessed with wanting to change others. As I began to feel the peace that comes from letting go, I began to make it through a whole day without obsessing about other people's actions.

Then when I prayed for God to grant me a sense of humor about myself, others, and life, he also answered that prayer. Into my life came Myra. Myra had her problems, too, but she had a sense of humor about life. She taught me how to laugh again—not at people or life, but with people and in spite of life.

When we pray to God for power in our lives, he always surprises us with his answers and the package they come in.

BLB

*WILL POWER = our WILLingness to use a
Higher POWER.*   —ANONYMOUS

An abscessed tooth involves an infection at the root of the tooth. In order for the inflamed area to heal, a dentist must perform a root canal.

Unfortunately, the first of several root canals for me was at the age of eight. I understood nothing about the root of a tooth. I remember asking the dentist if he could just give me a shot of novocaine and send me home. He gently explained that a shot would only stop the pain temporarily but would produce no healing. Even though I didn't understand the process, I placed my trust in the dentist and had my first root canal.

Many of us don't understand our pain. We have tried to numb the hurt through our addictions and dependencies, but like the novocaine, the anesthesia of addiction wears off, and we face our pain again. Dealing with our addiction also causes pain at times, but like the root canal, it produces healing for us.

We may not fully understand God yet, and we certainly don't know all of the procedures he will use to help us recover. Turning our will and lives over to his care allows us to begin the process of healing.

Anesthesia never solves our problems of addiction, but working the program does.

CSH

Have Thine own way, Lord! Have Thine own way!
Thou art the potter; I am the clay. Mold me and
make me after Thy will, while I am waiting,
yielded and still.   —ADELAIDE A. POLLARD

This hymn brings to mind a picture of the ceramic pieces my children used to bring home from school. They would sit in art class, rolling out the clay and sticking the pieces together to make bowls, animals, or vases, and then carefully put them in the kiln to bake. After they were finished they would proudly bring home their art as a gift for me or their father. We would look at this lifeless piece of clay and try to show the proper amount of appreciation for their creation.

As we look around us today, we see the wondrous creations that God has molded out of clay, put in the fire, and brought to life. We need to see ourselves as a creation of God, molded out of clay by his loving hands, tempted by the power of sin and brought to life, from destruction, by his gift of grace.

How glorious are the mighty hands of the Lord, to create life from clay.

BLB

Your words were found, and I ate them,
And Your word was to me the joy and
*   rejoicing of my heart;*
For I am called by Your name,
O LORD God of hosts.   —JER. 15:16

Nutritionists remind us that "we are what we eat." As a nation, we are becoming more conscious of maintaining a healthy diet. Eating good food will not produce results in one day. Health requires making changes in our lifestyle on a consistent basis.

Jeremiah said that "eating" God's Word produced joy in his heart. Of course, he was not referring to literally eating Scripture. We can develop an intimate relationship with God by spending time with him through meditation and prayer.

We may have wandered aimlessly for years when we were trapped by our addictions. Now we realize that the Bible provides a source of truth, which can direct us and guide us to an understanding of God's will for our lives. We can turn to God's Word for comfort and support as we struggle through the painful issues of recovery. It brings joy to our hearts when we realize that we are reading God's words to us. Draw strength from knowing that God has written to encourage you toward truth and freedom. Let us not minimize the power of God's Word in our recovery.

―――――――

Intimacy with God comes through spending quality time with him.
                                                              CSH

Jesus said to His disciples, "If anyone desires to come after Me, let him deny himself, and take up his cross, and follow Me."   —MATT. 16:24

In Twelve-Step programs, we often hear members talk about having "an attitude of gratitude." As you begin working the program you thought, *How could I ever be grateful for what has brought me to this program?* In time it will come. Remember that without the past, you would have no need to seek a healthier future.

Many people have overcome their past and changed the direction of their lives. One of my favorite stories is about Helen Keller. She had so many handicaps to overcome, but a spirit in her gave her the strength to be the best that she could be. Our handicap can be our attitude. We choose an attitude of self-pity, blaming our parents or being angry at our spouse. With this self-defeating attitude, we set ourselves up to be the loser.

As we work through our program of recovery and list the patterns we want to change, let's first work on changing our attitude. Make a list of the things we are willing to stop doing and another list of the things we are willing to start doing. When we ask for the Lord's strength, we are given the power to change.

We are limited by attitude, not by opportunity (Earnie Larsen).

BLB

*For He Himself has said, "I will never leave you nor
forsake you."*   —HEB. 13:5b

Loneliness is a natural human emotion. It can produce a feeling of deep despair or bring a gnawing pain
to our hearts. We can feel lonely even when we are
with a group of people. We feel the pain of loneliness
when we are isolated from ourselves.

When we grow up in dysfunctional families, we become confused about who we really are. We learn to
base our identity on how other people treat us. That
leads us to develop untruthful ideas about our signifi-
cance. As we become isolated from our true self, we do
not want to be alone because we do not like our own
company.

In recovery we can learn to accept ourselves. We
can learn that we are never really alone, because God
has promised to be with us always. We can allow God
to direct our lives as we turn our will over to his care.
As we know more about God and ourselves, we can be
comfortable with silence and time by ourselves. We begin to realize that we are never truly alone.

*I am never really alone, because God is always with me. I can find
happiness in being with God and with myself.*

CSH

"Come to Me, all you who labor and are heavy laden, and I will give you rest. Take My yoke upon you and learn from Me, for I am gentle and lowly in heart, and you will find rest for your souls. For My yoke is easy and My burden is light."
—MATT. 11:28–30

We often feel abandoned by God, but God never moves. When we feel alone and think that nothing is going right, we have moved away from God. To the alcoholic it can seem like nothing is going right. Financial problems plague the business. The children are having problems at school. The spouse is always yelling. Alcohol becomes a comforting friend, but it also causes problems at work and with the family.

Step Three is the opportunity to start over again. As we work the steps, we first admit only God has enough power to set things right. And second, we admit that the way we are living is insane. Now, with the faith of a child, we can put our life in his hands. Being willing to turn our life and our will over to God is the beginning of making things right again. In his hands we can receive the love and nurturing we so desperately need. In his hands we do not feel abandoned.

———

Pulling against the yoke of the Lord will only chafe your neck.

BLB

Don't quit five minutes before the miracle happens.
—ANONYMOUS

If you have ever stood on the beach and watched the ocean waves crash onto the shore, you know what an awesome experience it can be. The dancing waves intrigue us, as do the fascinating creatures found just below the surface. As we gaze upon its vastness and listen to the mighty roar of the waves, we have intense feelings ranging from power and strength to beauty and serenity.

Has it ever occurred to you that oceans are composed of tiny particles of water? Even the vast expanse of beach is formed by combining tiny grains of sand.

Slowly, but surely, step by step, small things that may seem insignificant combine to create something great and wonderful. We often feel discouraged by our small attempts to move forward in recovery. We focus on how far we have left to go instead of being encouraged by the progress we have made. Try to enjoy collecting each small experience along the way instead of fretting over when you will be farther along.

God, help me to enjoy the small steps, trusting that eventually you will produce a masterpiece.

CSH

> *"If anyone serves Me, let him follow Me; and where*
> *I am, there My servant will be also. If anyone*
> *serves Me, him My Father will honor."*
>
> —JOHN 12:26

We think of saints as those people who are next to angels in God's kingdom. But if we look around us, there are saints next to us right where we are. A saint I know is named Grace. Grace gets up before dawn on Sunday morning in order to drive more than forty miles to church. The reason she comes so early is to prepare the coffee. She then greets us with a warm smile and a fresh cup of coffee.

Faye also comes to mind. Faye suffered a stroke several years ago. Currently she suffers a very painful pressure sore. But every Sunday morning Faye is at church gathering people round her with her smile and friendly words.

Another saint is Ethel. Every Sunday morning, Ethel would visit her mother at the nursing home and then, as a minister's wife, she would be at the church with a smile and a warm word of welcome for each of us. She drops by with food when someone is sick and grieves with you when you are sad.

Saints are next to angels and angels next to God, so when we see a saint next to us in church or in the grocery line, then we must believe that God is right next to us too.

BLB

I can't handle it, God. You take over.
—ANONYMOUS

Recently, while in a recovery bookstore, I saw a T-shirt that read, "Everything I ever let go of had claw marks all over it." Many of us laugh as we recognize and agree with that sentiment. Our encouragement comes from learning willingness to let go, even though we don't necessarily want to.

Recovery never just happens. It is a long process, and we cannot grow toward change unless we are willing. There is a big difference between being willing and wanting. We all proved that by keeping our addictions to relationships, things, and behaviors because of our unwillingness to face the pain of change and because we wanted to continue in our comfortable habits.

Let's face it—whoever said, "No pain, no gain," spoke the truth. We may not always enjoy attending group meetings or going to therapy. Difficulties arise when we make amends with certain people. Discomfort increases as we struggle with forgiving those who hurt us. Still, the question remains: Are you willing to do whatever it takes to produce change, even though you may not want to?

Pain teaches us valuable lessons. Even in our pain, God is always with us.

CSH

"Take My yoke upon you and learn from Me, for I am gentle and lowly in heart, and you will find rest for your souls."   —MATT. 11:29

It is hard to have a relationship with people who are defensive, confrontive, and unpredictable. When you talk with defensive people, they either blame others or deny the facts. You ask them why they did something and they angrily say, "It wasn't me." Confrontive people catch you off guard. They come on at unexpected times and confront you about what you said, what you did, or what you did not do. In answering confrontive people you may feel angry, frustrated, or defensive yourself. You may want to run away from them. Unpredictable people can cause you much discomfort. They may be unpredictable in public behavior as well as in personal relationships. George, an alcoholic, has all three of these characteristics. He has driven his family away, hurt his relationships at work, and is still blaming others for his problems.

How do we deal with someone like this? First, we deny them the power to affect us. Second, we turn to God for the power to deal with them. Third, we become willing to let God work through us.

Doubt sees the obstacles; faith sees the way (Anonymous).

BLB

When all else fails, read the instructions.
                    —ANONYMOUS

When the car breaks down, we take it to the mechanic. If the plumbing gets clogged, we call the plumber. For most of the problems we encounter, there is a specialist we turn to for assistance. Why then, when we are confronted with a need that is beyond the capabilities of another human being to fix, do we turn to ourselves instead of to God?

The owner's manual for our complete care was written long ago by God himself. The Bible is full of Scripture exhorting us to lean on God for our well-being. Psalm 55:22 says, "Cast your burden on the LORD, and He shall sustain you." Proverbs 3:5 tells us, "Trust in the LORD with all your heart."

What can we expect once we make the decision to trust God with our will and our care? Philippians 4:6–7 tells us not to worry about things, but instead to pray about our problems. God will answer our prayers and provide us with a peace that is beyond human understanding.

———————————

God promises to provide us with the guidance, strength, and peace we need.

                                        CSH

*Therefore humble yourselves under the mighty
hand of God, that He may exalt you in due time.*
—1 PETER 5:6

Visualize a tall bearded man in a long robe, dusty from traveling, wearing sandals, with twelve friends straggling along with him. He knocks on your door and asks for lodging. How would you respond?

It would be a surprise to my family to come home and see them sitting around our dining room table. But what about the words our Lord said to us: "Feed my sheep"? It's okay to go down to the homeless shelter on Thanksgiving and serve hot meals to the less fortunate. We can adopt families for Christmas and gather clothing and food for them. We can put our money in the collection plate to help others. But would we invite Jesus and his friends into our home if they knocked on our door today? Would we tell our son that we are sorry we hurt him by saying something that put him down in front of his friends? Would we tell our spouse we are sorry we lost our temper over something he or she forgot to do? Would we admit that at some time our behavior shut someone out of our life when he or she was searching for a kind word?

Are we willing to invite Jesus into our world, or are we only willing to go out, at our convenience, into his world?

BLB

*If you don't surrender to Christ, you surrender
to chaos.*   —STANLEY JONES

Our culture stresses that we should be the master of
our fate and the captain of our soul. Society places a
high value on self-sufficiency. Pride is a human tendency that drives us to try to be in control. Believing
that we must always have total control becomes very
frustrating and self-defeating.

Our frustration eventually leads us into addictions
which are symptoms of our hunger for control. There
is an extreme paradox in addictions, because although
they are a result of our need to have control, the addictions are evidence that our lives are totally out of control.

Fortunately, God has provided a way for us to escape
from the tyranny and destructiveness of self. He has
graciously invited all of us to come to him for rest.
Psalm 46:1 says, "God is our refuge and strength, a
very present help in trouble." When we are willing to
stop trying to control, then we can turn our lives over
to God. He has promised to give us abundant peace.

*When I allow God to control my life, the chances are much greater
for reaching a healthy destination.*

CSH

But without faith it is impossible to please Him, for he who comes to God must believe that He is, and that He is a rewarder of those who diligently seek Him.
—HEB. 11:6

Hebrews 11:7–10 tells us about the faith of some well-known people in the Bible. Noah, by faith, built an ark for his family. And when the floods came, they all survived. Abraham, by faith, went out to receive his promised inheritance. Sarah, by faith, bore a son long after her childbearing years.

These people all lived by faith in the unseen and were willing to trust in God to deliver them. Our faith is weak because it is based upon stories of things seen. Our trust is in the known.

Though these people from the Old Testament did not live to see the promises they believed in, we can receive our promises by just being willing to put our lives in God's hands. The gifts we have been promised are love, joy, peace, longsuffering, kindness, goodness, faithfulness, gentleness, and self-control. We can receive them all by asking and by being willing to change our attitude to one of acceptance of God's gifts.

A miracle is seen when God is reflected in our life.

BLB

Nothing that is worth doing can be done alone,
but has to be done with others.
           —DR. REINHOLD NIEBUHR

Can you imagine the game of football without a coach for the team? There would still be eleven men on the team, but each player would be trying to do his own thing. Nothing would be accomplished, because no one would be working together. The team needs a coach who has a greater knowledge of the game than they do. He calls the plays so everyone knows the plan and works together.

We would be foolish to continue our struggle through the game of life without allowing God to coach us. He sees the big picture and knows the best ways to direct us. Although the direction he leads us may feel difficult at times, God always has our best in mind. He works through every situation to conform us to his image. Our goal in life is to become more like God each day.

God gives us a team for support in our Twelve-Step groups. We all work toward self-awareness, spiritual awakening, and recovery. Joining together for encouragement and allowing God to guide us leads us in the right direction.

I trust that God has everything under control.

                                                   CSH

Cast your burden on the LORD,
And He shall sustain you;
He shall never permit the righteous
    to be moved.   —PS. 55:22

When we struggle on our own, the task sometimes seems insurmountable. What a relief it is to "let go and let God" help us.

Many times I put things in God's hands, only to take them back again. For instance, I turn my children over to God and then proceed to tell God how to do his job.

One day I was sitting on the porch with my friend Elizabeth. I was telling her how unhappy I was over the way my daughter's life was turning out. She said, "I felt the same way about Kris, until one day the Lord spoke to my heart and asked me if I was pleased with the way things were going in Kris's life. I answered that I was not pleased. He then reached me with the words, 'Then why don't you step back and see what I had in mind for her?'"

I got the picture.

Our children are a gift from God. How we care for them is our gift to God.

                                        BLB

So he said, "I heard Your voice in the garden, and I was afraid because I was naked; and I hid myself."
—GEN. 3:10

There are times when we each feel alone and afraid, such as when we face unexpected surgery or experience the loss of a loved one. These feelings are normal during such circumstances. However, a problem arises when we feel ashamed in addition to feeling alone and afraid. Our shame can often be a healthy warning that we are stepping outside God's will for us.

The story of the first sin in Genesis tells us that before eating of the forbidden fruit, Adam and Eve were naked and were not ashamed. After eating the fruit they became alone, afraid, and ashamed, because they were apart from God. Their eyes were opened to the difference between right and wrong and to their nakedness.

We sometimes feel alone, afraid, and ashamed after we give in to temptation and do things that are displeasing to God. The healthy shame felt in a situation like that is actually God convicting us of wrong actions. By trusting in God as our Higher Power, we don't ever have to be alone, afraid, or ashamed again.

Healthy shame warns us when we are stepping out of God's will.
CSH

Therefore, if anyone is in Christ, he is a new
creation; old things have passed away; behold,
all things have become new.   —2 COR. 5:17

Many miracles happen through prayer. Relationships are healed, habits are changed, and hearts are mended. One Sunday, after I began working the Twelve Steps, I was sitting in church and as I looked at the altar I prayed:

God, I have accepted my powerlessness;
your power I need.
I have accepted my disbelief. In you I believe.
I am willing to give my life to you.
Now wash me with peace and make me clean.

As I sat there, a warm feeling came over me, just like when the sun warms you when it peeks through the clouds for a minute on a cloudy day. I felt strength, warmth, and most of all, a great sense of peace. My husband must have sensed that some change had come over me because he turned and looked at me. I felt my face had a radiant glow because that was the way it felt from the inside. He put his arm around the back of the bench and gave me a gentle hug. I knew then that miracles do happen. God had let his "Son" shine on me and give me peace.

Miracles are answered prayer.

BLB

> *"He who has begun a good work in you will complete it."*
> —PHIL. 1:6

My writing seems overwhelming at times. Fortunately, my husband David provides great encouragement. In those tough moments, he reminds me that God remains faithful and that he is in control. When I trust God for guidance and commit the project to him, despair turns into hope and I feel much less overwhelmed.

Fortunately, I am unable to just whip out a book in one short month. I would feel very arrogant and prideful about my own abilities. Obstacles that seem too large to overcome bring me to a place of weakness. God promises that in my weakness he remains strong.

Most of us feel weary at times when we face situations in work, relationships, and recovery that seem impossible to deal with. God desires to use those troubled moments as a way of pointing us to him. When we accept our own inabilities, we can allow God to take control of our lives. He promised to finish the good work he started in us.

As we meditate on Scripture, the Word enables us to live in a way that is pleasing to the Lord.

CSH

I lay down and slept;
I awoke, for the LORD sustained me.
I will not be afraid of ten thousands of people
Who have set themselves against me all around.
                              —PS. 3:5–6

The past few weeks I have felt a lot of stress. I come home tired, and when I try to get all the tasks accomplished that I set out to do, I don't seem to have enough time. One evening, as we were preparing dinner, I mentioned to my husband all the work I had to do before bedtime. He pulled me over to him, put his arms around me, and said, "I want you to slow down. You are important to me, and I don't want you to wear yourself out."

That must be what God tries to say to us when we enter church: "I love you and I want you to take care of yourself. Come unto me and I will give you rest."

It was a wonderful feeling that evening to know someone cared enough about me to confront me in a loving way. The rest of the evening we spent enjoying each other's company. The next morning I awoke refreshed and ready to get back to work. Believe it or not, I got more done that day than I ever hoped to accomplish.

Accept God's offer of love and rest. Of all life's gifts it is the best.
                                                    BLB

The roots grow deep when the winds are strong.
—CHARLES SWINDOLL

One of the greatest blessings in my life has come from my relationship with my grandparents. Their strong character and moral fiber were formed through great hardship. They shared memories with me of hard labor, loss of jobs, years of depression, and the death of a child.

Their bodies grow frail now, but when I look at them, all I see is strength. They remind me of majestic oak trees that have grown strong and tall through years of storms. Just as the tree sends down deep roots to stabilize itself during heavy winds, so too my grandparents have become anchored by roots that grew securely in godliness.

Many of us feel like an oak sapling when it comes to storms! We can offer thanks for the strong winds, because when things go too smoothly, we don't feel such an urgency to allow God to have control.

During difficult times we can sink our roots into God's strength.

CSH

Trust in the LORD with all your heart,
And lean not on your own understanding;
In all your ways acknowledge Him,
And He shall direct your paths.
  —PROV. 3:5–6

When I was a little girl growing up I heard the expression, "You have to learn from experience." I'm sure my mother would have preferred that I learn from her instruction, especially the first time she said it, but I preferred the hard way—experience.

This attitude continued all through my school years. I always had to try it to believe it. Needless to say, it got me in trouble on occasion. One time I decided to change my name. The way I did it was to just start turning in my papers with my new name on them. After an "experience" with the teacher, I learned that was not the way to do it.

Good things have come from my experiences too. I was given a job at the church to do. I went into it not knowing exactly what to do. A year later I had learned many things from the experience.

Life is made up of instructions and experiences. We can learn equally from both if we are willing to listen and to participate.

What we learn from others, others learn from us.

BLB

Blessed is he whose transgression is forgiven,
Whose sin is covered.   —PS. 32:1

Guilt is a luxury to a recovering alcoholic. It cannot be afforded. That is why the Twelve Steps of Alcoholics Anonymous allows for a daily self-examination, confession, and repentance of any wrongdoing.

Carrying guilt around for years is physically, emotionally, and spiritually damaging. Your body can suffer from many physical disorders. Emotionally, you become depressed, antisocial, and lonely. Spiritually, guilt drives us away from God and into despair.

Johnny tried to escape the stress and physical problems brought on by guilt by turning to alcohol and drugs. He was always in trouble as a child. That was the only way he could get any attention. His parents neglected him at home and he found out that if he acted up at school, he would get some much-wanted attention. Always being in trouble was painful, though, and he had to find some way to comfort himself.

Our recovery from guilt comes by accepting that Jesus came, not to remind us of our sin, but to forgive us our sins.

———————————

Once God forgives, he forgets.

BLB

Do not be conformed to this world, but be
transformed by the renewing of your mind,
that you may prove what is that good and
acceptable and perfect will of God.

—ROM. 12:2

One's attitude makes a difference in how one behaves. How do you feel about your life? Is it exciting to
get up in the morning, dress, and go about your business, or do you dread the drudgery of the same old
thing?

Mary complains about being tired all the time. She's
angry with her mother for being around all the time,
but she says the children are too much trouble for her
to handle all alone. She says that her husband never
does anything with her, but when he asks her to go
somewhere with him, she complains she doesn't have
anything to wear or feels she cannot leave the children. Some days she just wants everyone to get out of
her house and leave her alone. When she is alone, she
complains about being lonely.

There are solutions to this despair. God provides us
with the opportunity to change our attitude. When you
recognize what God's will is for you, then your attitude
will change towards your circumstances.

You are only as happy as you choose to be.

BLB

We made a searching and fearless moral inventory
of ourselves.

We can be blind to our own faults but see clearly the
faults of another. In the Twelve-Step program, we call
that taking someone else's inventory. When you point
your finger at someone else, look carefully at your
hand. Three fingers are pointing back at you.

When Sue and John came in for counseling, they
spent the whole first session telling about the things
they wished the other one would change. Once I got
them to repeat to each other what they were hearing, they realized how they sounded. They were only
looking at each other's faults and not at their own responsibility to the marriage.

As we ask God to open our eyes, what are we willing
to see? Do we dare stand in front of a mirror and ask
God to reveal our true self to us, when we spend most
of our time denying who we really are? We say we
wish to serve the Lord. How willing are we to serve
when it interrupts what we are doing and when what
we are called to do is not to our liking?

Lord, open our eyes to see you more clearly and to see ourselves as
you see us.

BLB

> *Therefore let him who thinks he stands take heed
> lest he fall.*
>   —1 COR. 10:12

Recently Katie returned to Overeaters Anonymous and began to work the Twelve Steps. Having reached a low point emotionally and spiritually, she felt her only options were suicide or total surrender to God.

She chose to turn her eating over to God's control. Daily Katie prayed for wisdom in eating food that would nurture her body and not harm her. Her weight began to decrease, and she thought her desire to compulsively overeat had vanished.

Then a subtle change began to occur in her thinking. Katie started saying, "I'm not *really* a compulsive overeater. Weight loss just requires determination and willpower. I'm doing great!" Maintaining a cocky attitude led her into bingeing again. She took her focus off God as her source of power. A proud attitude about her own self-discipline led her away from seeing her need for God.

Proverbs 16:18 says, "Pride goes before destruction, and a haughty spirit before a fall." We must admit that we need God's power on a daily, or even hourly, basis.

We never have to rely on our own strength and self-control. God is faithful to carry us every step of the way. He will never fail us.

                                                            CSH

For as he thinks in his heart, so is he.
—PROV. 23:7

As we grew up in dysfunctional families, we heard things about ourselves that were not true. Maybe nothing we did was good enough to please our parents. Maybe we were constantly told that we were stupid or an accident, or maybe we were abandoned or abused, which made us feel worthless and unlovable.

We are not responsible for the abuse we received as children, but we are responsible for how we choose to live as adults. The Bible says that knowing the truth will set us free. Many of us have no freedom because our brain works like a tape recorder that continues to play back the lies of the past. Believing those lies keeps us in bondage to poor self-esteem.

Begin now to accept that God made you as a precious and unique creation. He delights in loving you. Listen to your self-talk and confront the lies from your past with this truth. If you have difficulty deciding what is the truth, ask yourself if the belief brings you freedom or if it feeds your damaged self-image. Only truth produces freedom.

———————

Today I will try to encourage myself with the truth.

CSH

*Let each one examine his own work, and then he
will have rejoicing in himself alone, and not in
another. For each one shall bear his own load.*
                                        —GAL. 6:4–5

Do you sometimes feel that things are not working
out for you? Relationships with people at work, family, friends, spouse, and God may be strained. Look at
those relationships to determine what pattern runs
through all of them. Is it a pattern of stepping back or
of being too forward? Is it a communication problem?
Is it a problem of talking too much or not enough? Perhaps it is in your expectations. Maybe you want everyone else to do all the work.

In working on improving relationships the easiest
one to begin with is God. He is always there, he loves
us unconditionally, and he is a great listener. When he
does talk to us, it is through all our senses.

Next we begin improving our relationships with our
family. In this relationship we have to risk being more
vulnerable and open to feelings. With friends we can
learn to be there for someone else, to be vulnerable to
their needs. Loving ourselves is also a relationship that
we need to improve.

---

*If we see ourselves reflected in the love of God, then we are able to
risk reflecting that love to others.*

                                                        BLB

*And we know that all things work together for
good to those who love God.*   —ROM. 8:28a

In the program, we are told to "let go" and "turn it
over." We work to stop controlling the people, places,
and things in our lives. Even though we may not want
to let go, we work toward willingness to give God control. Sometimes we believe that once we turn our lives
over to God, only good and wonderful things will
happen.

We feel upset when life continues along as usual.
Loved ones still get sick, accidents happen, and fi-
nances remain a struggle. We may feel that God forgot
us, and that our letting go did not work.

Some of the things that occur in our lives are not
caused by our issues of recovery. Many of the incidents
are just life. Some things that happen now have nothing to do with what happened in our past.

God shows his love for us by using even hurtful
events in our life and eventually creating something
good out of them. The program gives clear evidence of
negative turning to positive. We begin in brokenness,
and we grow to the point of sharing our story to encourage others in their healing process.

*God's timetable is different from ours, but we can trust that he is
working for our benefit, even in hard times.*

CSH

Commit your works to the LORD,
And your thoughts will be established.
                          —PROV. 16:3

When I was a little girl we had a housekeeper who teased me, saying she was going to wash all my badness away. What a wonderful idea! We could fill a big bathtub with hot water, sprinkle in some detergent and swish it all around, and then climb in and wash that badness away.

Jesus taught us an easier way. All we have to do is (1) recognize our sin, (2) confess it to God, (3) turn from the sinful behavior, and (4) accept God's forgiveness. Jesus' method lasts forever.

We use the Fourth Step to recognize our sins by making a fearless moral inventory of ourselves. When we confess these sins, God promises us a way back from destruction. In repentance, we redirect our lives and go in another direction. As we look to God, we know that only by his love and forgiveness have we been saved from death.

———————

God washes away my sins and makes me just as if I'd never sinned.
                                                          BLB

I will fear no evil;
For You are with me.
—PS. 23:4

Peering into a mirror, we look at the reflection of ourselves. We cover what we perceive as flaws through the artistry of makeup or with the use of wigs or toupees. Some things cannot be changed, and through the course of time we learn to accept these areas. In much the same way, we need to look inside ourselves and accept both our good side and our dark side.

Our good side poses no problem, and we easily embrace and display our best qualities. On the other hand, our dark side is often difficult to face. We try to hide this painful inner part from others because we fear rejection. If we deny the existence of our hurts and refuse to deal with the problems we create, then tragedy awaits us through continued addictions.

A journey through our darkest places feels painful and scary, but the search must be made. Psalm 51 tells of David going through such an investigation. David said in verse 6, "You desire truth in the inward parts, and in the hidden part You will make me to know wisdom." The promise of God is to be with us always. Let us learn to put our trust in him.

"The unexamined life is not worth living" (Socrates).

CSH

*Just as He chose us in Him before the foundation of
the world, that we should be holy and without
blame before Him in love.*   —EPH. 1:4

Even before we were born, God had a plan for us. As
children we may have dreamed of what we wanted to
be when we grew up—a doctor, nurse, lawyer, fire
fighter, parent, or teacher. We all wanted to be well
liked. Today we may be a doctor, nurse, lawyer, fire
fighter, parent, or teacher. We may be liked by our
friends and family. Still we may feel all alone and out-
cast. We may have taken some wrong turns along the
way.

We should remember that God is in control. Even
before we were born he provided for us to be loved.
Jesus came to tell us about God's love for us. He even
told us that we all have made wrong choices at some-
time in our life. Jesus calls us to look at our sins, not
dwell on them. He tells us that God loves us, each and
every one, exactly where we are and who we are. In
his eyes we are perfect, because he loved us so much
that he forgave all our wrong choices.

Accept God's love and go through life knowing you are loved.

BLB

> *Let us search out and examine our ways,*
> *And turn back to the LORD.*
>   —LAM. 3:40

During the summer months, dandelions overrun our yard. In the past, I would spend hours pulling up these weeds. Weeks later, the same weeds would return in full force. Dandelions have a long root that has to be dug out of the ground. I put forth a lot of time and energy, but I merely broke off the weeds at the surface. The roots remained underground, and the weeds soon resurfaced.

We usually want to avoid looking at our root issues. We take care of the symptoms, but we are often afraid to look at the deeper problems. Step Four requires that we make a searching and fearless moral inventory of ourselves. Searching will mean digging deep to find our root issues. This will be uncomfortable, but God will lovingly guide us as we turn our lives over to him.

Issues, like dandelions, only go away when you dig out the roots.
                                                              CSH

> *"Forgive us our debts,*
> *As we forgive our debtors."*
> —MATT. 6:12

People can choose between good and evil because God gave us free will. Our base inner nature leads us to evil, so sin becomes a way of life.

God loves people. We are his children. Just as we tell our children not to do something and then they do it, God tells us not to sin but we do. As we struggle to discipline our children, God struggles with us. If we let our children establish their own rules, we would know frustration. They would choose to go to bed when they wanted, eat all the candy they wanted, take everything for themselves, and walk the road to destruction.

God loved us by setting rules for us to live by, but we still struggled with doing what God wanted us to do. He sent his son to wipe out sin by suffering the punishment for us. In dying, Jesus conquered sin and set us free. If we believe this, then we are free from sin and free to be with God in eternity.

Let us strive to forgive others as our Father has forgiven us.

BLB

"For it would have been better for us to serve the Egyptians than that we should die in the wilderness."
—EX. 14:12b

Moses obeyed God by leading the children of Israel out of the land of Egypt. Their journey would lead them to a promised land that flowed with milk and honey. The only problem was that the trip included being pursued by Pharaoh's army, walking in the wilderness, and wondering where they would find food and water at times. During each hardship the children of Israel complained with anger toward Moses. They desired to return to slavery, because at least in Egypt they knew what to expect.

We often act like the children of Israel. Our recovery will lead us to a promised land of healing for our damaged emotions. Yet whenever we struggle, hurt, or face hardships, we want to return to our old coping mechanisms, because even though they caused pain, they were predictable.

Let us learn from the mistakes of others. Slavery to old habits is a continual path of destruction.

Recovery may be painful at times, but our journey is leading us to a much more peaceful way of life.

CSH

A man's pride will bring him low,
But the humble in spirit will retain honor.
—PROV. 29:23

The need to do a searching inventory of ourselves is not something to approach only once in a lifetime. It is something that helps us when looking for a job, entering a new relationship, or just learning to live with ourselves.

You can take inventories on different aspects of your life—your marriage, your relationship with a son or daughter, or your work relationships. You can do these inventories in chronological order, starting with the beginning of the relationship, or you can just write about specific events. When you describe an event, describe the behavior of the people involved. As you write, you will begin to see patterns of impatience, selfishness, anger, or abuse. You can also see other patterns in your behavior, actions, and reactions. From this you can list what was good and what you want to change. You can change any behavior you want. Choose the behavior and practice it "one day at a time" for twenty-one days. At the end of twenty-one days check yourself and see how you have done.

The faults that bother us in others usually bother us in ourselves also.
BLB

Pain is inevitable. Suffering is optional.
—KATHLEEN CASEY THEISEN

The body has a way of dealing with splinters we don't pull out. Soreness increases as the damaged area becomes inflamed and festers in an attempt to push the foreign object out of the body.

During our lifetime we may receive and collect a variety of emotional splinters. We often keep these hurts hidden away in our hearts for years. Some of the splinters were painful, like the physical, sexual, or verbal abuse we received in our homes. Others slipped in unnoticed, such as broken promises or events we participated in that our parents didn't attend.

Whatever the culprit may have been, years of denial and compulsions have allowed those hurts to grow and fester. We have tried to numb our aching hearts with addictions. We may have had no control over how those wounds got there, but we are now responsible for allowing God to help remove those hurtful splinters and restore us to wholeness.

I will allow God to give me insight into past hurts so that they can be removed.

CSH

He who keeps instruction is in the way of life,
But he who refuses reproof goes astray.
                              —PROV. 10:17

We are so busy trying to keep people from knowing who we really are that we eventually reach a point where we don't even know who we are. We give power to others by letting their impressions of us matter more than what we think of ourselves. We get to know ourselves in the Fourth Step.

Begin to get in touch with who you are by asking yourself questions about what interests you and what you don't like. Defensive people, rainy weather, and interruptions can cause us stress if we don't like them. Under stress we may take out our feelings on others.

Once, a man I know was videotaping his family. His voice was picked up in the background and he heard the sarcasm come out of his mouth. It really frightened him, because he remembered the pain he felt as a child when his father said sarcastic things to him.

Sometimes we need to step back and look in a mirror. Be objective in looking to see what others see. We need to know when we are giving freely because we have an interest in the other person and when the issue is one of control disguised as love.

When love is given freely, we get back more than we receive.

                                        BLB

In the midst of winter, I finally learned that there
was in me an invincible summer.
—ALBERT CAMUS

The intensity of winter weather varies depending on where you live. Trees stand dark and barren, grass and flowers turn brown and die, and often snow covers the ground. In gardens across the country, flower beds filled with bulbs for daffodils, tulips, and gladiola are dormant and cold. Imagine for a moment that these bulbs could identify feelings. They would surely tell of hopelessness, depression, isolation, and fear, to name a few.

Yet, each year, something wonderful occurs, called spring. The land begins to grow warm, the days become longer, and old things grow again with new life. Within a few months, those bulbs have produced an abundance of new growth and are blooming in brilliant colors. They decorate our homes and gardens and bring hours of delight to many.

Like the bulbs, we may face long periods of fear, loneliness and despair, but God desires to renew our heart with the healing warmth of new life through recovery. Look with hope toward the beauty that will be produced in your life.

God, give me courage to hope for springtime in my own life.

CSH

When I was a child, I spoke as a child, I
understood as a child, I thought as a child; but
when I became a man, I put away childish things.
For now we see in a mirror, dimly, but then face to
face. Now I know in part, but then I shall know just
as I also am known.   —1 COR. 13:11–12

When it comes to taking a personal inventory, we may have trouble getting started. At first we may think that we have to write down all the bad things about ourselves. But taking inventory really means taking a close look at our strengths and weaknesses.

Laura is competitive. She always wants to win. Being competitive is healthy, but when winning becomes a compulsion and stands in the way of friendships, it can be damaging.

Julie is too flexible. Being flexible is healthy, but being too compliant can be an unhealthy way to behave in relationships.

Compulsive personalities have a tendency to extremes. The extreme in behavior is the weakness.

You only have one life to live, so strive to live it in the best possible way.

BLB

An insult is like mud: it will brush off much easier after it dries.   —ANONYMOUS

The powerful emotion of anger may be used to protect or to destroy. Habits we used to produce excitement or to avoid pain have been motivated by self-destructive anger. Possibly in periods of rage we screamed damaging words of abuse, and later we mourned because they could not be taken back.

As we go through the process of recovery, we become aware of a new form of anger. This anger surfaces as we identify specific areas of abuse we endured. We need to be careful not to express our anger towards others in abusive ways and not to regress into our former patterns of hurting ourselves. We may face an overwhelming desire to confront those who hurt us.

Confrontations may be helpful if they are handled at a later time once we learn a healthy assertive manner. When the feelings first surface, we sometimes want to lash out at others, but that would cause more pain. Take time with your anger. If necessary, count to ten, twenty, or one hundred, or wait several days for your feelings to settle. Remember, it's easier to remove mud after it has had time to dry.

Trust today that God and time are on your side.

CSH

You shall not hate your brother in your heart. You shall surely rebuke your neighbor, and not bear sin because of him. You shall not take vengeance, nor bear any grudge against the children of your people, but you shall love your neighbor as yourself.
—LEV. 19:17–18

We may have heard growing up that anger is wrong. However, God was angry with Adam and Eve, and he expressed his anger by driving them out of the Garden of Eden. Jesus was angry with the money changers in the temple. He turned over their tables, freed the birds, and drove them out. In this sense it is good to be angry with evil and wickedness.

In Ephesians, however, Paul tells us that anger can be sinful too when it is born of selfishness. We sin when we get angry at someone who doesn't do what we want them to do, or when we express anger unfairly.

We must be wise and deal with our anger in a constructive way. If we suppress anger, it can make us physically or emotionally sick. If we vent it on others, it will be destructive to relationships. Learning to be angry at the problem but loving and caring to people is a constructive way of dealing with anger.

Love people; hate sin.

BLB

*That the genuineness of your faith, being much
more precious than gold that perishes, though it
is tested by fire, may be found to praise, honor,
and glory at the revelation of Jesus Christ.*
                                    —1 PETER 1:7

Gold goes through the process of refinement by exposure to extreme heat. The high temperature causes the dross to rise to the surface of the molten metal. This rubbish is then skimmed off. The process of skimming off the rubbish continues until the gold reaches the level of purity desired.

We often feel intense pressure during our moral inventory. Rubbish from our past rises to the surface. Recalling these memories and writing them down produces pain. We worked for years to suppress our feelings, and we resist digging them up.

God does not plan to hurt or damage us, but the purification process brings pain. We move further in recovery by working to identify and remove the damage from the abuse and addictions of the past.

God wants to make us more like the Lord Jesus. He never takes away anything positive or beneficial to our recovery. When God leads us through the fire of refinement, he only burns out of us those things that harm us and are not Christlike in nature.

Even in our pain, we trust that God is making us more like himself.
                                                        CSH

> *"Abide in Me, and I in you. As the branch cannot*
> *bear fruit of itself, unless it abides in the vine,*
> *neither can you, unless you abide in Me."*
> —JOHN 15:4

We have all received gifts. Like the people who were given talents in the Bible, we have used some and hidden others.

Often when we begin looking at ourselves we only see the faults. Still, each of us is unique and we each have special gifts. We need to search fearlessly for those gifts and make a list of them.

At our church we have people with many different talents. Mary is a very friendly person. She loves to talk with people, and she has the ability to make people feel welcome. John has a gift for motivating others. Mary Ellen can gather a crowd when there is a job to be done and make the crowd think they are having fun. Christine is quiet, but her gift is one of being able to pay attention to detail and organization. Harold has the gift of leadership, and Sandra works best on a team. Others sell, some buy, some make, and some fix. We all have gifts to use.

Jesus spoke of himself as the Vine and us as branches of the Vine. We all work, as we spread out from the Vine, but the Vine is our support and our nourishment.

In conducting your inventory, search for your gifts and then use them.
BLB

Life is difficult.
—SCOTT PECK

Fairy tales led us to believe that the beautiful princess is always rescued by the knight in shining armor, and then they live happily ever after. We grow up believing that the more successful we are in life, the easier it will be. Obviously, we aren't doing well if life is difficult.

The truth is that life is not easy, no matter how successful we are. Life will always be full of job losses, car wrecks, and poor health. If we continue to embrace the lie that life should be easy, we will grow to be resentful and bitter. We may even begin to question our faith in God.

God never promised us that life would be carefree. He promised to give us strength to face difficult times, and he reassures us that he brings good out of bad circumstances.

Once we learn that life is hard, we are no longer shocked when things seem unfair. We learn to accept difficulties as a chance for us to grow by allowing God to be in control.

_____

We rest securely knowing that even in difficult times, God desires to take care of us.

CSH

All the ways of a man are pure in his own eyes,
But the LORD weighs the spirits.
Commit your works to the LORD,
And your thoughts will be established.
                                        —PROV. 16:2–3

I have a friend named Myrna who is a wardrobe coordinator. Her job is cleaning out people's closets and then helping them fill them back up again. Twice a year Myrna comes over and takes a look at my closet. Now, this is scary to let someone in your closet, but Myrna attacks my old, wornout, faded clothes with relish. She makes one stack of clothes to give away, another to put up for the next season, and what is left over she lays out to match with blouses, skirts, and jackets.

Taking your personal inventory is something like this experience with Myrna. You open yourself up for soul cleaning. On one side of the page you write down all the things you want to get rid of. Then you make a list of your strengths. Some of these strengths may be like last season's clothes that need to be taken out, dusted off, and given a fresh look. The weaknesses we want to get rid of. Other characteristics may need to be given to someone else, like our caring, or our talents used to bring happiness to others.

Finding our faults is easy. It's changing them to strengths that is difficult.

                                                            BLB

*In the arena of human life, the honours and
rewards fall to those who show their good
qualities in action.*   —ARISTOTLE

One of my friends who works on issues of codependency in relationships also struggles with multiple sclerosis. MS progresses in stages and can cause loss of coordination and make even walking painful. Sometimes she feels "sick and tired of being sick and tired." Yet, she attends meetings even when she cries all the way there because she doesn't feel like going. She firmly believes that God desires her to be available, so she presses forward.

Most of us don't have to deal with a physical disease while we are working through our dependencies. Just the emotional pain we face from dealing with our addictions may feel defeating at times. When our distress feels unbearable, we may be tempted to leave the program or return to our addictions. Remember that those addictions also brought pain, and that the pain of recovery is a positive pain that will produce healing in our lives. God desires for us to be available to him even when we are hurting.

Availability means that we remain accessible to God so that he can be in control of our recovery.

CSH

*"Therefore if you bring your gift to the altar, and
there remember that your brother has something
against you, leave your gift there before the altar,
and go your way. First be reconciled to your
brother, and then come and offer your gift."*
—MATT. 5:23–24

As we begin Step Four it is important that we look not
only at our behavior, but also at our feelings, attitudes,
and thoughts. Stop for a minute and think. Are you
mad at someone right now? Have you let what someone else did make you angry? Have you stewed about
it until you are bitter and resentful toward that person?

I heard a story about two brothers who fought before bedtime. Their mother told them to make up before they went to sleep because Jesus might come
during the night. One of the brothers agreed, but said,
"Okay, I'll forgive him, but if Jesus doesn't come to-
night, I'm going to sock him in the nose tomorrow."

Forgetting a wrong done to us is as important as forgiving. God forgets what we confess to him, and we
are told by Paul that we are to forgive "that your Father
in heaven may also forgive you" (Mark 11:25).

---

*You must first make peace with yourself before you can make peace
with others.*

BLB

How poor are they that have no patience.
        —SHAKESPEARE

Many of us remember feelings of anger or confusion from our childhood when things did not happen quickly. It was difficult to wait for Christmas, difficult to hit the baseball with the bat, or difficult to understand mathematics in school. When things seem difficult, we become frustrated quickly and want to give up.

Our society stresses the importance of instant results and immediate gratification. We have difficulty learning the importance of taking recovery "one day at a time." Sudden growth in the program will be an exception to the rule. Our recovery requires that we persevere with patience. As unique individuals, our recovery and relief start at various stages in the Steps. It may take time for many of us to begin to feel stronger. We can draw encouragement from understanding that there is no set timetable for recovery. Our progress will occur at the appropriate time for us.

I need to be patient and accept the reality that recovery requires work and time.

                                        CSH

Let us search out and examine our ways,
And turn back to the LORD.

—LAM. 3:40

When we were children and something happened that was threatening to us, we behaved in a way to defend ourselves. These behaviors became defenses whenever we felt afraid and we used them for our survival. As a child, during stressful circumstances, these behaviors saved our life. Continuing them today, as adults, can ruin our relationships.

One patient lost her father suddenly when she was only two years old. Three months later, her mother delivered another baby girl. Shortly after that the mother had an emotional breakdown. This young girl faced major traumatic separations close together, and she shut down her emotions for protection. Her fear of being abandoned and her feelings of loneliness were so overpowering, that as an adult, she would rather not risk vulnerability. The more she stuffs her feelings, the harder it is for her to keep her feelings under control. Today she acts out her feelings on her husband and children in abusive ways.

We cannot expect another to be there for us all the time, but as a child we needed that security. Today, as adults, we have God for that security.

Receive the love and security God is offering you today.

BLB

*There is therefore now no condemnation to those
who are in Christ Jesus.*   —ROM. 8:1a

As we begin the process of taking inventory of our
past, many of us feel overwhelmed by guilt. We walk
around waiting for God to send down a lightning bolt
to strike us as punishment for our wrongs. Any time
something painful happens to us, we interpret it as
punishment.

It is important to learn the difference between punishment and consequences. The Lord Jesus took the
punishment for all of our sins when he gave himself as
the perfect sacrifice through his death on the cross. He
paid the penalty for our sins. When we place our faith
and trust in his completed work of redemption, we
need no longer fear punishment.

We do need to be aware of the fact that some of our
actions will produce painful consequences. Scripture
makes this clear. "For whatever a man sows, that he
will also reap" (Gal. 6:7). If we plant corn, we produce
a harvest of corn. If we have planted seeds of addiction, we will reap some painful consequences. The
truth remains that God does not punish us for our behaviors, but we often face the natural consequences of
our deeds.

*When the consequences are painful, we can look to God to provide
comfort for our hearts.*

CSH

Blessed is the man who endures temptation; for when he has been proved, he will receive the crown of life which the Lord has promised to those who love Him.
                                        —JAMES 1:12

Children who grow up in a home where their childishness is not accepted as normal develop a survival system. This survival system is their defensive reaction to the five- and six-foot giants who rule their world. In the children's minds, they had to rationalize the adult's behavior. The behavior could have been chaotic, confusing, unstable, and even violent. There had to be some acceptable reason for the unacceptable behavior, so the children learned to deny reality. The reality was the sickness of the adults. The denial was the children's words, "It must be my fault." They could cope with their behavior, change it, adjust to it, or do whatever they needed to do to survive, but they could not cope with blaming their life-support system. As these children grow up, their denial system stays intact. They need it for protection from the chaos of the adult world.

The beginning of overcoming this defensive nature is to trust in God. There is no chaos in God's relationship with us.

—————

We wear many masks, but God sees us as we truly are.

BLB

I can't . . . God can . . . I think I'll let him.
                        —ANONYMOUS

Most of us can handle the first three steps, but the idea of taking a moral inventory produces extreme anxiety! Some people choose to stop their recovery at Step Four, because they fear confessing the inventory to themselves. Putting our past down on paper seems to make it overpowering.

We turned our lives over to God so that we are now able to draw strength from him. Remember that God already knows everything about us. He is very familiar with both the good and bad. Our inventory will not offer God any new and alarming information about us. God did not harm us during our active addictions, and now that we are in recovery, he is not going to be upset by things he already knows.

We gain a better understanding of ourselves as we examine our past behaviors. We have developed many protective barriers that have kept us from knowing ourselves and from being in touch with our feelings. We can go forward knowing that the purpose of the inventory is not to keep us stuck in the past, but to move us toward a healthier future.

The past is a historical tool that can help me gain understanding of my current behavior.

                                        CSH

There is no fear in love; but perfect love casts out fear, because fear involves torment. But he who fears has not been made perfect in love.
                                    —1 JOHN 4:18

What is your major fear? We can usually identify our fear if we look at what we deny, ignore, or avoid. Isolating ourselves from social settings is avoidance of a situation that we fear. Maybe we fear the attention or maybe our fear is that we will be rejected, ignored, or unaccepted. Perhaps we fear making decisions. Maybe we don't have enough confidence in our ability to decide on something as important as a future career, marriage, or even where to live. Maybe our decision is over something as mundane as what to wear or whether or not to buy something. When we fear change or the unknown, we use denial to mask our fear. If we deny the need to change or if we deny what could be, then we don't have to face our fear.

We need to learn to trust our feelings. The perception we have of ourselves is more important than the perception others have of us.

_____

When we trust in the Lord, our realities become less fearful.

                                                    BLB

We admitted to God, to ourselves, and to another human being the exact nature of our wrongs.

Keeping secrets makes us sick. As a child we quickly learned the rules: don't talk, don't feel, don't trust. We don't tell others what happened at home, because we fear they won't like us. We kept the secret that Daddy didn't really have the flu when he stayed home from work. We hid the reason Mother couldn't come to the school program. Sometimes we even learned to lie when someone asked us how we felt and we replied, "Fine. How are you?" Inside we hurt.

Promises were made and broken, we felt scared or unhappy, and others told us we did not feel that way. We began to rely on others to tell us how we felt.

In recovery, we can choose how we want to feel. We can talk to our sponsor and others in the program as we learn to trust them. At meetings we can begin sharing those secrets that made us sick.

Share your burdens to make them lighter; share your joy to make it more fun.

BLB

*I will praise You, for I am fearfully
and wonderfully made;
Marvelous are Your works,
And that my soul knows very well.*
—PS. 139:14

Whenever I hear the word *rejection,* I see a quality-control worker standing next to a conveyer belt covered with peaches. That person's job requires pulling out all of the peaches that are bruised, cut, or damaged. This fruit is unacceptable for the consumer.

We often use the word *rejection* to describe what someone else did to us when they ended a relationship or to describe how we felt as children if our parents were emotionally absent. We tell ourselves that we are like the worthless peaches that are tossed aside. We believe that someone rejected having a relationship with us because we were not acceptable.

However, God tells us that he made us in a wonderful way. He loves us so intimately that he knew all about us before we were ever born. We may have suffered through abuse in the past, but that does not make us unacceptable.

No one has the power to reject us, but each of us has the freedom to make choices about our relationships.

CSH

> *"I say to you that likewise there will be more joy*
> *in heaven over one sinner who repents than over*
> *ninety-nine just persons who need no repentance."*
> —LUKE 15:7

Jesus told a wonderful parable of a shepherd who owned one hundred sheep. One of the sheep got lost, so he left the ninety-nine and went in search of the one lost sheep. The shepherd kept looking until he found his sheep.

He did not punish or scold the lost sheep. Scripture says he rejoiced and carried the sheep home to safety. Jesus concludes that there is more joy in heaven over one person who repents than there is over ninety-nine who have no need for repentance.

Our addictions isolated us and caused us to feel lost. Step Five helps us remove the barriers that kept us away from others. We admit to God, to ourselves, and to another human being the exact nature of the wrongs we discovered in the Fourth Step.

Finding a safe person to hear our inventory is necessary. This person needs to be trustworthy and unbiased about what we desire to share. Confession helps to purge out the anger, shame, fear, and grief that crippled our lives.

_____

God lovingly carries us home and restores our relationship with him.
CSH

We also glory in tribulations, knowing that
tribulation produces perseverance . . . and
character, hope. Now hope does not disappoint,
because the love of God has been poured out in
our hearts by the Holy Spirit who was given to us.
—ROM. 5:3–5

When Suzanne thinks back about things that happened in her childhood, feelings of sadness, shame, guilt, or loneliness surface. She did not know what to do with her feelings back then. Sometimes as an adult she feels sad, ashamed, guilty, and lonely. She still doesn't know what to do with these feelings. She came to group therapy at the clinic for help.

Her story has a happy ending. She found out that God made each of us because he wanted to share all the beautiful things he had made in the world with those he created in his own image. He gave us freedom of choice, and when we chose evil, he provided for forgiveness in the nature of Jesus Christ.

Simple? Yes. So simple a child can understand that when they do wrong, the hugs and kisses that follow the discipline are forgiveness from a loving parent. When a child does not have forgiveness, it is hard to understand this concept, but through Christian counseling, they can come to believe in the love and forgiveness of God.

_____

God hates sin but loves the sinner.

BLB

We are only as sick as our secrets.
—ANONYMOUS

Glenda learned to keep many secrets. Her father threatened her continually throughout nine years of incest. When she began recovery, she had blocked out her childhood and was only aware that she felt depressed.

Now, a year into recovery, Glenda shared her story with her support group. She understands her true feelings about the past. Each time she shares her secrets, they lose the power to control her. Bringing the secrets out in the open sets her free from the bondage of hiding her pain.

Most dysfunctional families keep many secrets. Unspoken rules tell us never to let others know what happened in our home. We may feel guilty when we first begin to share our secrets from the past. We must remember that keeping secrets hurts us. The secrets form abscessed wounds in our hearts, and we move into our addictions to try and stop the pain. As we voice the secrets, they lose their power over us, and our hearts can begin to heal.

I will be entirely honest so that no secrets or lies can stop my recovery.

CSH

"Be angry and do not sin": do not let the sun go
down on your wrath, nor give place to the devil.
—EPH. 4:26–27

Living in a dysfunctional family is cause enough for having angry feelings. The dysfunctional system provides many threats to your emotional and physical survival. How you deal with your anger about these threats is the most important element of your survival. In *Patterns of Communication,* Virginia Satir says that threats create stress and we need to learn to effectively cope with this stress in order to survive. How do we do this when it has not been modeled for us and we haven't learned it as a behavior?

Anne came to counseling to learn. When she was under stress she blamed her husband, distracted herself with work, or exploded in a rage at everything that went wrong. After she exploded she would feel so bad that she would turn her anger on herself and become very depressed. Anne learned through counseling that she could not change or control others, but she could change and control her behavior. She began by admitting to and taking responsibility for her part in the stressful situation.

How do we learn what was not modeled for us in childhood? We teach ourselves.

BLB

"The lamp of the body is the eye. If therefore your eye is good, your whole body will be full of light."
—MATT. 6:22

In the Thornton Wilder play, *Our Town,* a character named Emily has died. She receives the opportunity to return and relive one day of her life. Choosing her twelfth birthday, Emily returns to her family. She becomes overwhelmed by the realization that people seem blind to one another. They rush through life and don't take time to really see the preciousness that each person possesses. Emily tearfully begs her mother to look at her for just one minute with no distractions. The blindness of her family becomes too painful, and Emily begs to return to her grave.

We rush through life so quickly that our vision becomes blurred. We miss priceless moments of life because busyness, introspection, and addictions distract us. People and things become invisible.

Working in recovery helps us gain restored energy to focus on the preciousness of human life. We begin to see ourselves and others in deep and appreciative ways. We can relax and focus on the many simple pleasures and beauties of life.

Let us ask God to touch our eyes, remove our blindness, and teach us to see clearly with our hearts.

CSH

Examine yourselves as to whether you are in the faith. Prove yourselves. Do you not know yourselves, that Jesus Christ is in you?
—2 COR. 13:5

As I was driving to church this morning I saw a young blind woman making her way down the sidewalk towards a church. I marveled at her progress as she tapped her cane, identifying the path she needed to follow. I remembered how I had gotten up early, read the paper, dressed, and jumped in my car to rush off at the last minute to attend my Sunday school class. It was really effortless on my part, but still I was running late. And here was a young woman making every effort she could to attend her church.

How many of us with sight see less than the blind woman? How many of us with two feet stumble as we walk the path of Christ? How many of us fail to put Christ first in our life? The power of the Lord dwells in each of us. The power to bring sight to the blind and happiness to the sick of heart exists in each of us. Think of all the people you rushed past and did not see because your eyes were looking down rather than upward. Stop and look around you. People need your love and your kindness.

Sometimes it seems impossible to change ourselves; how could we ever change another?

BLB

> *Trust in the LORD with all your heart,*
> *And lean not on your own understanding;*
> *In all your ways acknowledge Him,*
> *And He shall direct your paths.*
> —PROV. 3:5–6

Yesterday, I picked up an old book of my mother's, and when I opened it, some papers fell out. I looked at the few words written on the papers and that brought back some wonderful stories. One of them reminded me of a story I heard many times about a neighbor down the street who jogged early in the morning. As he ran, he would toss my parents' paper up on their front porch. Mama and Papa weren't in good health, so it was convenient for them not to have to go down the steps and out to the front sidewalk to pick up the paper.

Another piece of paper had some names written down with "thank you" beside the names. I am sure these were people who had done something nice for Mama, and she always called or sent a note of thanks.

The third piece of paper was a grocery list. This is the paper that really made me stop and think. I thought, *Why can't we write out a list for God, asking for patience, kindness, and joy?* We could also make a list of our problems and give them to Jesus.

Lists help us remember kindnesses we have received and problems we wish to shed.

BLB

We can help one another find out the meaning of
life. But in the final analysis, each is responsible
for finding himself.   —THOMAS MERTON

Although Nathan viewed himself as defective, in school he excelled in sports and academics. His father remained passive, and although he never criticized his son's performance, he never offered praise either. Nathan interpreted his father's silence as rejection. Nathan grew up believing that he lacked some mysterious quality, and that if he could ever attain that quality, his father would show him love and praise.

In order to resolve the conflicts and hurts of the past, Nathan needed to learn the truth about himself. The fact that his father was silent and withdrawn said something about his dad, but nothing about Nathan. His lovability and self-worth were not based on his father's actions. He was not lacking or defective.

His recovery involved learning to accept himself and being satisfied with his abilities. He learned to use positive self-talk to encourage himself, and he allowed God's love and acceptance of him to heal the wounds of the past.

_____

God made each of us as his precious creation!

CSH

"As I was with Moses, so I will be with you. I will not leave you nor forsake you."   —JOSH. 1:5

Joyce Landorf, a noted author and lecturer, speaks of God's waiting room. This is where we go while we wait for God's answers.

Janie is in God's waiting room at this time. She is a single parent with two teenagers who had become involved with drugs. They have both been through treatment and are now in aftercare. Janie is attending Al-Anon and working her program. She has to let go of the problem and let God work through her. She is in his waiting room praying for physical, emotional, and spiritual healing for herself and for her children.

When we go to God's waiting room, God is with us. Sometimes he answers our prayers with a yes, sometimes with a no, and sometimes he answers with a maybe or a not now. But God cares about us and he hears us. He has given us a book that has words of comfort for us. In this book he says to us, "Lo, I am with you always" (Matt. 28:20).

God tells us to look within ourselves; that is where his power works miracles.

BLB

"But the very hairs of your head are all numbered."
—MATT. 10:30

At times we may feel insignificant and believe our life is meaningless. Within us lies a deep longing to feel cherished, important, and significant.

Jesus described in Matthew 10:29–31 how he desires to care for us. He explained that two little sparrows were sold for a penny, and yet God knows each time one little bird dies. He encourages us that we are of much greater value to God than a sparrow. God is so intimate with us that he even knows the exact number of hairs on our head. Now that makes us significant!

God knows everything about us, and he still chooses to love and accept us. He knows each of us in a deep, personal way, and he desires that we in turn would seek to have a meaningful spiritual relationship with him.

No human will ever know us as intimately or cherish us as much as God does. He is our Creator, and he designed us to be complete only when we have a personal relationship with him.

_____

Since God's eye watches even small sparrows, we can rest assured that he watches over us with great care.

CSH

*So when they continued asking Him, He raised
Himself up and said to them, "He who is without
sin among you, let him throw a stone at her first."*
—JOHN 8:7–9

Many times I have sat in front of the fire on New
Year's Eve, reflected over the past year, and made resolutions for the new year ahead. So many of the resolutions are the same ones year after year.

The Twelve-Step program teaches us to take one day
at a time, one change at a time. Each day as we say the
Serenity Prayer, asking for the serenity to change the
things we can, we take a mental inventory of our
strengths and weaknesses. As we go through the day
we call on the Lord to help us with our inventory. God
knows that just like our New Year's resolutions, our
daily inventory is going to crop up with the same items
from time to time. He offers us the opportunity to
come to him in prayer in the evening, asking his forgiveness for our weaknesses and praising him for our
strengths. We end the day putting the inventory list in
his hands. He allows us to be free to start all over the
next day with a new list.

One choice at a time, one change at a time, one day at a time.

BLB

Instant gratification isn't fast enough.
—UNKNOWN

Our society stresses doing things in the shortest amount of time. We have instant foods, microwave cooking, thirty-minute workouts, and even gimmicks for weight loss while we sleep. If there's an easy short-cut, we're all for it. That idea can cause confusion in our recovery. We want to hurry up and get it over with.

We attend seminars, read self-help books, and listen to any personal improvement tape we can find. We want healing in one afternoon, and we want someone else to do it for us.

It's okay to dream about the future, but it's un-healthy to believe we'll get there with no effort. If we could buy recovery, there would be no need to medi-tate or to submit ourselves to God.

Changing requires action. We must plan for im-provement and practice the principles for recovery on a daily basis. _____

I will work the program one step at a time.

CSH

*That we should no longer be children, tossed to
and fro and carried about with every wind of
doctrine, by the trickery of men, in the cunning
craftiness by which they lie in wait to deceive.*
                                        —EPH. 4:14

Jesus came to call us to work for his ministry. To do
this we show our love for the Father, others, and ourselves. We show our love for the Father by reading the
Bible and attending church. We show our love for
others by our service to them. But how do we show
love for ourselves?

When Jennie came to counseling she was depressed, lonely, and hurt by the way people abused
her. After weeks of therapy she came to realize that
she brought on her depression by constantly putting
herself down and expecting perfection in all that she
did. She also brought on her own loneliness by isolating herself from others because she found relationships too controlling and too painful. Others abused
her in the same way she abused herself. They criticized
her, put her down, expected perfection in her performance, and rejected her when she did not do things
the way they thought she should. Now Jennie is recovering by learning to love and to take care of herself.

Do to yourself as you want others to do to you.

                                                    BLB

Don't care FOR, care ABOUT.
—ANONYMOUS

We often become confused about the difference between caring for someone and caretaking them.

As caretakers, we rescue others from facing situations that will cause them embarrassment or discomfort. We do for them what they could easily do for themselves. This allows us to feel good about ourselves, because we feel needed and in control. It enables the people we rescue never to take responsibility for their own actions. They become dependent on our caretaking and never learn to take care of their own needs and feelings. We help them become emotionally retarded.

Caring for others means that we let go of them. We accept them as they are, and we stop trying to change them. They have the freedom to make mistakes, take responsibility for their behavior, and then learn from the experience.

Caring offers encouraging words and a hand to help us up when we fall. A caretaker tries to remove the obstacle before we ever have a chance to stumble.

Be kind to others, but give them the freedom to make their own mistakes.

CSH

Thus says the LORD:
"Let not the wise man glory in his wisdom,
Let not the mighty man glory in his might . . .
But let him who glories glory in this,
That he understands and knows Me,
That I am the LORD, exercising lovingkindness,
*   judgment, and righteousness in the earth.*
For in these I delight," says the LORD.
                                    —JER. 9:23–24

Gwen made a resolution to go on a diet. In fact she has made many resolutions to diet. She suffers from the "yo-yo" diet syndrome. She does fine until she skips a meal, and then she binges. Afterwards she feels guilty because she broke her diet. Instead of going back on the diet, she comforts herself with food. Now Gwen is suffering not only the pain of guilt but physical pain from nutritional imbalance.

The anger Gwen feels at herself for her behavior drives her deeper into depression. Her whole self-image is affected because she feels that her job depends on how she looks. How she looks depends on what she eats. What she eats depends on staying on her diet.

This is called the cycle of addiction. To break the cycle she needs to be open and honest about what she thinks and feels. Learning why she eats is the basis for recovery.

_____

God, give us the strength to attain lasting success in all our endeavors.

                                                        BLB

*The man who makes no mistakes does not usually
make anything.*   —EDWARD PHELPS

Although he did not realize it, John viewed himself as
a saint. He never thought he would have premarital
sex, but he did. He sat in my office and questioned how
this could happen. His view of himself had switched
from wonderful to terrible.

The truth is that sometimes people behave in wonderful ways, and sometimes they behave in terrible
ways. Most of us behave both ways at different times.
We distort reality when we view ourselves in all-or-
nothing, black-or-white extremes.

Denial and pride set John up to fall. His arrogance
made him unaware of a weak area in his life. He
needed to work on having a more balanced, truthful
view of himself.

Our arrogance leads us to see ourselves as terrible.
We set ourselves apart as unique, because we view
ourselves as worse than everyone else. None of us is
uniquely good or bad. We each fall somewhere in the
middle, and that makes us human. Our own humanity
points out our need to allow God to control our lives.

———————

Put aside uniqueness and welcome yourself to the human race.

CSH

If you have been foolish in exalting yourself,
Or if you have devised evil, put your hand on
your mouth.
For as the churning of milk produces butter,
And as wringing the nose produces blood,
So the forcing of wrath produces strife.
                                        —PROV. 30:32–33

Some of us carry a lot of baggage full of memories from the past. One suitcase may be our anger at another person's behavior. The anger may be our reaction to broken promises, unfair treatment, or verbal put-downs. Nevertheless, the anger got packed in a suitcase and we still carry it around with us. Maybe another suitcase contains fear of another's anger, fear of abandonment, or fear of physical pain. The fear stems from the past but you still carry it around with you today. Guilt for your past behavior may fill the third suitcase. Here again, the suitcase you carry is full and feels heavy to carry.

No wonder you feel tired and weighted down! You carry a heavy load. Set the suitcases down and begin unpacking them. You need to talk with a friend, minister, or counselor in order to get it all out. God forgives us even before we ask, so he washes away the anger, fear, and guilt during prayer.

Travel light and see the sights.

                                                          BLB

Let all bitterness, wrath, anger, clamor, and evil
speaking be put away from you, with all malice.
And be kind to one another, tenderhearted,
forgiving one another, just as God in Christ
also forgave you.   —EPH. 4:31–32

Johnny said that as a child he had a hard time learning how to do things. He was taught not to hit, bite, or kick. But when he got mad he wanted to do all those things, especially when he was defending himself. He was hit often by his father, who drank too much. Now, as an adult, he has a hard time expressing his anger. He still feels like hitting when he is angry. Sometimes he does.

The anger, resentment, and desire for revenge is understandable if children have been abused by their parents, but to live with it for years after the abuse makes them unhealthy. Johnny needs to let go of the feeling for revenge. He needs to see his father as a very sick man. Johnny needs to stop hanging on to what has happened in the past and move forward by working to forgive.

Just for today, I can do anything that will bring me the peace that I so desperately seek.

BLB

Though I have the gift of prophecy, and understand all mysteries and all knowledge, and though I have all faith, so that I could remove mountains, but have not love, I am nothing.   —1 COR. 13:2

When Martha was growing up, she felt very little power as a child. Her father was an alcoholic, so his behavior was very unpredictable. She never knew when she came home from school if he would be there drunk, sober, or even there at all. He would make promises to her and then never keep them. She learned to take care of herself because she could not depend on anyone else to be there for her.

As an adult, she has an intense need to control her life and her feelings. She also needs to control others around her. This gives her the sense of predictability she needs. Unfortunately, this obsession with control destroys the ability to be spontaneous. It also leaves one unable to trust others. They feel they must have a hand in everything that is going on and they trust only themselves to complete projects or to handle situations. Becoming aware of this need to control others, accepting the past, and changing what we can change lead to peace and serenity.

When I feel a need to control another, I will seek the power to control myself.

BLB

"You shall have no other gods before Me."
—EX. 20:3

We can compare an addiction to a false god. An addiction can creep up on us, and before we know it we have found a means of relieving our pain. The pain is caused by loneliness, guilt, or feelings of low self-esteem. We become obsessed with the pain, and then we become addicted to what relieves the pain.

Carol's addictions were spending money, drinking alcohol, and eating. One evening she and her husband had an argument on the phone. She was out for the evening with a friend and thought her husband was out of town on business. When she called home to get her messages he answered. The argument started, she hung up, went to eat with her friend, and drank beer until she was drunk. The next day, when she came in to see me, she did not feel well emotionally or physically. Addictions rob us of our own power. We become powerless and do things we wouldn't normally do. Our compulsive nature is insane.

God offers us a way to get out of bondage to these addictions. We just need to be willing to turn our life and our will over to him. If something or someone comes before God, that is a false god.

Confess your addictions to yourself, to God, and to another human being, and then turn from them.

BLB

> *Progress always involves risk.*
> —MARY R.

If we think back on our closest friendship, we may remember a time when our friend took a risk and shared openly about the pain in her life. She was probably embarrassed as she unveiled some of her moral failures. Her greatest fear at that moment was of being rejected for daring to take the relationship deeper through self-disclosure. Yet, most of us felt honored that our friend would dare to trust us with such secrets. Hearing of weaknesses did not repulse us. Our friend's vulnerability made her more dear.

Many of us fear sharing our inventory with someone else. It produced enough pain just to admit it to ourselves. We believe that we will face rejection, but each of us has done things about which we are ashamed and embarrassed. As we begin to openly share these incidents, we realize that people in our group still love and need us. Their knowledge of our past failures will not change their feelings of love for us.

Step Five brings us the healing gift of joy as we see that others accept us.

CSH

The steps of a good man are ordered by the LORD,
And He delights in his way.   —PS. 37:23

The more stressful life becomes, the more some of us are driven to handling stress in unhealthy ways. Sarah is a competitive person. She wants to achieve, so she pushes herself to perform at top efficiency. When she gets involved in a project, she forgets about time and becomes totally absorbed with what she is doing. Then when she is reminded to stop and attend other responsibilities, she feels stressed out. Her compulsion to work on only one project at a time creates stress when there are several things that need attention at the same time.

We all attempt to deal with stress in many different ways. We blame others for creating stress for us. We keep it inside us and let it create physical distress. To overcome this we can learn how to set realistic goals, plan and organize our time, and follow the AA slogan "Keep it simple."

By planning ahead and relying on the power of God rather than acting impulsively, we can gain a healthier way of dealing with stress in our life, thus eliminating the unhealthy ways we handle stress.

Through prayer we have the power to change.

BLB

Grow in the grace and knowledge of our Lord and Savior Jesus Christ. To Him be the glory, both now and forever. Amen.   —2 PETER 3:18

A young bird leaves the nest when he learns how to fly. Due to his lack of experience with the ground, he still requires plenty of help in locating food. Eventually the young, helpless bird will mature and learn to feed not only himself but also his offspring.

As we enter recovery, we experience a new freedom as we leave our nest of addiction and learn to trust God's power to guide our lives. Even though we may find new independence, we remain like the little bird who still needs feeding. Our spiritual food will come from spending time with God by reading the Bible and praying. We are greatly nourished by talking with our sponsor and interacting with members of our group. We gain strength and insight as we trust God and follow the examples set for us. As we work the steps, we learn more about ourselves and mature so that we can search for truth and apply it to our own lives.

Eventually we grow to a place of teaching others what we have learned.

CSH

And many who had believed came confessing and telling their deeds.
                                        —ACTS 19:18

We learn from experience. The outcome of every thought, word, and deed we experience teaches us how to think, speak, and act in the future.

Carolyn wishes that she could run an instant replay of some particular incident, in order to evaluate what was said and how she reacted. We learn from others, and when we experience stress, we react in the same way that we saw someone else react. Carolyn wants to learn a healthier way to act under stress instead of just reacting. She is doing this by practicing healthy attitudes and behavior one day at a time. In this way she is taking care of herself and recovering from self-defeating thoughts and irrational behavior.

Growing up is accepting responsibility for your thoughts, words, and actions. With God's guidance we can all become the best that we can be.

                                                    BLB

*A friend is one who knows all about you and loves
you just the same.*   —ANONYMOUS

Upon entering the program we felt isolated and
unique. Surely no one else faced our same experiences
and hurts. As people in the program began to reach
out to us, we learned that they truly did understand us,
and we realized that we are not alone. We learned by
listening to others in recovery and watching their
actions.

Friendships are a necessary part of our recovery. Because we all need other people, making friends is one
of the most important activities in our recovery. Learning to share with others and care about their concerns
helps us not feel alone in a crowd. We feel a sense of
belonging in the program that we had desired for a
long time.

We need to remember that each person we meet
brings something new to teach us. Learning this truth
helps us to honor each individual. Whenever we reach
out to someone in pain, we carry the message of hope
for recovery. We should always remember how good it
felt when we first entered the program and someone
reached out to us.

*We must work the program for ourselves, but we certainly can't do it
without the help of our friends.*

CSH

*"I say to you that likewise there will be more joy in
heaven over one sinner who repents than over
ninety-nine just persons who need no repentance."*
                                        —LUKE 15:7

Maybe the same thing keeps happening over and
over in your life. You enter relationships with people
you care about, but you just can't seem to get close to
them. You have everything you could want—a wonderful spouse, three children you love, and a nice home—
but you feel unhappy. Or maybe things seem to
suddenly fall apart in your life. You hurt and don't
know why.

   Growing up in a dysfunctional family we experienced conditional love and unpredictable behavior. Today we cannot blame others; we need to take
responsibility for our lives. We need to bring the patterns of self-defeating behavior into our conscious
mind, look at them, recognize the feelings that go with
them, and then change our behavior to a healthier pattern. The power to do this comes from God.

Our past affects us, but with God's help we can change the future.
                                                    BLB

And Jesus answered and said to them, "Those who are well do not need a physician, but those who are sick."
                                              —LUKE 5:31

We wear masks every day to keep people from knowing us. Shyness is a mask we wear, hoping to be invisible. Maybe we hide behind a mask of caretaking. Taking care of others, making all the decisions, and dominating conversations are all ways to control a situation. Controlling gives us a sense of power we did not have as a child. We also wear masks to protect us from hurt in intimate relationships, cover our inferiority complex, or make us feel better than others. Many of us wear the mask of Goldilocks: we're always searching for just the right person, thing, or event to make us happy or give us comfort.

Living behind these masks becomes more difficult as we get older, but we are afraid to take them off. We fear that if others knew us they would abandon us. Still, continuing to wear the masks keeps us apart from intimate relationships. It is risky taking our masks off with another person, so it helps to get to know ourselves first. As we love, nurture, and care for ourselves we begin to feel safer in letting others get to know us.

We can only grow up one day at a time.

                                                    BLB

> *"Be angry, and do not sin": do not let the sun go*
> *down on your wrath, nor give place to the devil.*
> —EPH. 4:26–27

A mother took her child to the park one afternoon. Within a few minutes she heard a shriek that she recognized. She turned to see the neighborhood bully punch her son. The abuse that took place made her angry, and she ran to pull the larger boy off her son. The anger she felt was motivated by her love for her son.

Some of us believe that we deserved the abuse during our childhood. Believing these lies keeps us from dealing with the hurt and anger in our hearts. We often stay in abusive relationships as adults because we are used to it and we feel that we don't deserve better treatment.

Healthy forms of anger protect us. Our self-esteem grows as we learn to express anger motivated by love for ourselves. We learn the truth—that we did not then and do not now deserve to live with abuse. Working through the anger and grief of our past is a major part of our recovery.

———————

Anger which is motivated by genuine love provides a healthy frame of protection.

CSH

And the son said to him, "Father, I have sinned against heaven and in your sight, and am no longer worthy to be called your son." —LUKE 15:21

Children are born hopeful, trusting, believing, and willing. As these babies grow up they experience anger, greed, and distrust. They learn these things from us, for we are the world. If we live with fighting, we teach anger. If we give into our compulsions, we teach greed.

When God made Adam and Eve he gave them freedom of choice. He told them, though, not to eat the fruit of the Tree of Good and Evil. Because of their freedom of choice, they chose to disobey God. They ate the forbidden fruit and suffered by living a life of war, greed, and distrust.

We have the same choice today. Do we live in obedience to God, or do we choose to eat the forbidden fruit and live a life out of the realm of peace and serenity?

Awareness of the choices we make in our life is the first step toward recovery. Willingness to work on the problems is the solution.

BLB

We were entirely ready to have God remove all
these defects of character.

A man went to the doctor and found out that he had rabies. He immediately pulled out a pad and pen and began to write frantically. The doctor explained that there was no need to write out his will because he was not going to die. The man quickly responded that he was not making out a will, he was writing down a list of people he was planning to bite!

Some of us spend years waiting to get back at people. We keep a mental list of people that we plan to "bite" the next chance we get. We waste a lot of energy keeping our anger fueled and ready for attack.

Holding a grudge in our hearts breeds bitterness. Carrying resentment is like dragging around a fifty-pound anchor. It tires us out and steals the joy of living. Bitterness damages us more than the people we are angry with. To grow in our recovery, we must let go of our past grudges and move forward to the joy of living each new day.

Joy returns when we throw away our grudges.

CSH

Blessed are the poor in spirit,
For theirs is the kingdom of heaven.
Blessed are those who mourn,
For they shall be comforted.
                              —MATT. 5:3–4

When Gloria was nine years old her mother died. Gloria didn't know her mother was going to die; she just knew she was supposed to be good and quiet because her mother didn't feel well. The day they took her mother to the hospital, Gloria didn't even kiss her good-bye. She was busy playing with a friend. Her mother never came back, and Gloria grew up thinking it was because she didn't kiss her good-bye. Gloria felt her mother didn't love her enough to come back home, because Gloria wasn't good enough.

Gloria grew up with a need for love, but she also had a drive to be good enough so that those she loved wouldn't ever leave her. Because of the pain of the loss, she was afraid to ever love completely again, for fear of losing the ones she loved. As Gloria reached adulthood she used food to comfort herself. Now, through prayer, Gloria seeks the spiritual strength to stop using external things to comfort herself and to find healthier ways to behave.

_____

We do not have to reach outside ourselves for comfort. Peace lies within us.

                                              BLB

*Yes, we had the sentence of death in ourselves, that
we should not trust in ourselves but in God who
raises the dead.*   —2 COR. 1:9

Living with abusive, addictive behavior causes a family system to become sick. Members of the family develop their own symptoms of the disease based on the
defenses they use for survival.

Mary withdrew, repressed her feelings, and denied
all that was going on. In doing this she became emotionally unavailable for her spouse and her children.
Her husband was hanging on to his addiction for survival because that was the only way he could feel comforted for the pain his behavior brought him. The
children adapted to whatever role they needed to play
for the survival of the family. In doing this they de-
fended themselves and their right to be here.

Johnny, the son, was the super-responsible hero. He
saw that everything ran smoothly and perfectly. Ann,
his sister, felt the need to make everyone happy. She
would act out in order to get attention. Each of these
behaviors leads to dysfunctional relationships as
adults.

---

*We can only change by admitting and taking responsibility for our
role in a dysfunctional family system.*

                                                    BLB

*I am responsible for myself; my recovery, my
well-being, my happiness, all these things are,
ultimately, my own responsibility.*
—ANONYMOUS

Many houses in our neighborhood have tall wooden
fences around their backyards. Each fence marks the
property line and sets a boundary to keep other people
out. It would seem a little strange if one person in the
neighborhood had a habit of peering over fences to
take inventory of what each family keeps in their yard.

Each of us has an emotional backyard where we
store all of our motives and feelings. Many of us avoid
dealing with our recovery issues by focusing on what
other people are keeping as hidden agendas and emotions. What other people have in their "backyard" isn't
any of our business, but we certainly would rather focus on other people instead of ourselves. It seems
safer, but we don't grow any or learn to take responsibility for our own feelings and actions.

*Focus today on your own issues, and let other people take care of
their own "backyard."*

CSH

For the message of the cross is foolishness to those who are perishing, but to us who are being saved it is the power of God.
               —1 COR. 1:18

Perfection only describes our Lord Jesus Christ. We are imperfect, which means we have made some mistakes.

I have always loved the story of the football player who made so many mistakes just before the half that he made it almost a certainty for the other team to win the game. He wanted to dig a hole and cover himself up with dirt. He sat in the corner of the locker room during halftime. He knew he would be benched for the rest of the game and never be able to redeem himself. As they were leaving the locker room to return to the field, the coach walked over, touched his shoulder, and said, "Roy, show them how you can play ball."

In forgiving us, God sends us back into the game to try again. Faith is what we rely on when there is no factual evidence that we won't make another mistake. Hope keeps us in the game.

In our imperfection we move away from God. In his perfection he is always with us, loving us, forgiving us, and giving us hope.

                         BLB

"My grace is sufficient for you, for My strength is made perfect in weakness." —2 COR. 12:9

As adults we have a prideful attitude that children don't have. Children ask for help because they have enough wisdom to know they need it. We have great difficulty putting aside our pride and simply asking God to be in control.

God desires that we come into a relationship with him with the heart of a child. Being childlike requires admitting our helplessness in many areas of life. We must recognize our need for guidance from someone who knows more than we do.

God promised that when we are weak, he remains strong. When we become empty of ourselves, he can fill us with his strength and wisdom. Just as loving parents delight in taking care of their child, so God finds great joy in providing direction for us.

We come before God in Step Six to willingly ask him to remove our addictions and dependencies. As we hold up the deficits of our character before God, we can rest assured that there will be no condemnation. He will receive us as a loving parent and will provide the strength we need to continue to move forward in recovery.

_____

I will view weakness as a positive pathway toward seeing my need for God's strength.

CSH

Let no corrupt communication proceed out of your
mouth, but what is good for necessary edification,
that it may impart grace to the hearers.
—EPH. 4:29

It is said that listening is 75 percent of communication. Gloria said that if that is true, then as a child she really learned to communicate. Finding someone to sit and listen to her just talk about how she felt or what she was thinking was very rare. She spent her time just listening. She grew up in an alcoholic home. Because no one would listen, she felt very unimportant. Resentment welled up in her and she carried this over into adulthood.

When she came to the clinic for counseling, she did not trust anyone, she behaved in ways to get attention, and she would destroy relationships for fear she would get hurt.

Today, she is learning to express her feelings in an open and honest way. Not only is she letting others know what she thinks and how she feels, she is being honest with herself. She is feeling better physically and socially, and as her relationships improve her stress diminishes.

———————

You cannot be angry at someone and at peace at the same time. Deal with your anger in a constructive way as soon as possible and then let it go.

BLB

> *My soul melts from heaviness;*
> *Strengthen me according to Your word.*
> —PS. 119:28

The other night several of us talked about depression. Someone asked, "What do you do when you're depressed?" I stopped to think about this question a moment and then replied, "I go for a walk."

In Texas, you don't have very many days when you can't go for a walk. If the weather is not just right, wait a few hours and it will change. In Texas you can have snow, rain, and sunshine all in one day.

When I walk, I hear birds singing and I look up and see a beautiful sky. I notice that you never see the same sky twice. The clouds are different, or the time of day and the time of season are different. I feel the air on my face and I smell the freshness of the new morning or feel the warmth of a sunny afternoon. There is no way to go for a walk and not feel God's world all around you. We may not see him or hear him, but we will feel his presence.

When we walk in God's world, we feel him walking along with us.
                                                              BLB

*I am not responsible for my feelings—only for what
I do with them.*   —DR. CEOPHUS MARTIN

Having grown up in an abusive family where no feelings were allowed, Jane did not know about her own
emotions. She felt deep pain in her heart and sought to
silence it with food. Jane started recovery two years
ago, and she is slowly losing weight.

Two months ago she found out that her closest
friend was moving to another state. She panicked and
wanted to withdraw from the relationship in order to
avoid the hurt of saying good-bye. After discussing the
situation with her therapy group, she stayed in the
friendship and allowed herself to experience the sadness of losing her friend.

When we acknowledge our inner child and begin to
listen to our feelings, our self-esteem grows. We feel
valuable. We give ourselves the attention and affirmations that we needed during childhood but did not receive.

Jane and her friend spent special time together sharing their feelings and appreciation for each other. Now
Jane allows herself to cry each time she needs to
grieve. She feels sad but not depressed, because she
lovingly accepts the emotions instead of trying to
avoid them.

---

*Today I will embrace my feelings and acknowledge them as one of
God's gifts to me.*

CSH

*Be anxious for nothing, but in everything by prayer
and supplication, with thanksgiving, let your
requests be made known to God.*   —PHIL. 4:6

For the last six years I have attended a Bible study.
Each year at Thanksgiving the leader tells a story
about managing our time. She holds up a jar half full of
rice and in the other hand she holds a bag full of twelve
golf balls. The rice represents the everyday activities
in our life—car pools, meetings, dinners out, cooking,
packing lunches, work, letter writing, errands, and so
on. The golf balls represent the spiritual activities in
our life—one for prayer, one for church attendance,
one for Sunday school, one for daily Bible reading, one
for teaching our children about Jesus, and so on. They
represent the things we say we are going to do on Sunday and wonder why on the next Sunday that we
haven't gotten them done.

The leader shows us how to fit the golf balls (spiritual
life) into the jar half full of rice (everyday activities).
Only a few will fit. Then she empties out the rice, puts
all the golf balls in the jar, and then pours the rice in.
The rice filters down into all the spaces left between
the golf balls.

---

*If we put spiritual activities first, there will be room for the everyday
activities.*

BLB

Be yourself. Who else is better qualified?
    —FRANK GIBLIN II

Luke was raised in a rigid Christian home and church where he had unknowingly lived out the Twelve Steps. He was admonished to judge every sin in his life (real or imagined)—Step Six. Luke was taught that he was nothing compared to God, so humility was no problem—Steps Two and Seven. Prayer and meditation were musts—Step Eleven. So entering a Twelve-Step program seemed like nothing new to Luke.

What was new was his underlying motivation for living the program. In the past, Luke performed the Twelve Steps with robotic precision. He detached from his feelings and behaved acceptably. His church and family supported and fed this dysfunctional "Christian model."

In recovery Luke is learning that God cares about who he is and what he thinks. God wants emotional honesty as well as outward conformity.

For those of us with frozen emotions, God wants to be a safe harbor for docking our pent-up pain. For those of us on an emotional roller coaster, God wants to be a gentle stabilizer.

God gives dignity to who we are emotionally.

                                                          CSH

> *"For if you forgive men their trespasses, your heavenly Father will also forgive you. But if you do not forgive men their trespasses, neither will your Father forgive your trespasses.*
>
> —MATT. 6:14–15

Carrie finds forgiving others a most difficult thing to do. When she feels hurt by what someone says or does she wants to strike back. Many times the other person doesn't know they have hurt her, but she feels devastated. She conjures up all sorts of revenge as she lays awake at night rehearsing the conversation where she will tell them off or get even. In the meantime, the tension required to hold onto that anger affects her physically as well as emotionally.

The Lord helps here by telling us, "in whatever you judge another you condemn yourself" (Rom. 2:1). He encourages us to make peace with our brother before we come to the altar to worship him. He tells us anger is sin. We need to confess our sin and receive the Lord's forgiveness rather than wield that power over others.

We do not forgive because the other person deserves forgiveness; we forgive because we deserve freedom from anger.

BLB

In my end is my beginning.
—T. S. ELIOT

Old western movies make surrender look like an easy step. The outlaws merely tied a white handkerchief to a stick and waved it around in the air. Surrendering to God so that he can remove our defects of character seems very difficult.

Many of our habits became "comfortably uncomfortable." We grew accustomed to using our habits to cope with our problems, even though they produced pain in our lives. At times we felt as if the habits helped us to survive.

We may feel a great amount of grief as we start to let go of these behaviors. Even though we now understand that our old behaviors produced pain, they protected us for a long time. As you allow yourself the freedom to grieve, remember that healing has begun and recovery can last forever.

God desires to replace our old habits with healthy behaviors.

CSH

But now after you have known God, or rather are known by God, how is it that you turn again to the weak and beggarly elements, to which you desire again to be in bondage?   —GAL. 4:9

Our group members are all learning healthy, more balanced ways to live. Barbara wants a more balanced emotional life. She has had one relationship after another go wrong. She is practicing healthier ways of communicating her thoughts and feelings. Sarah wants a more balanced spiritual life. She is working the Twelve-Step program and attending a Bible study. John is codependent. He is learning to reach inside himself for comfort rather than depend on someone else to fulfill his needs. George is addicted to school. He has multiple degrees and is a very intelligent young man, but his life is out of balance. He is working on using his knowledge and skills to find work outside the classroom. Marsha is addicted to jogging. She runs ten miles a day, enters every marathon she can, and works out as often as possible. She says that running gives her meaning in life. She is working on finding meaning in a more balanced way, taking into consideration her work, family, and health.

When we call on the power of God to give us the peace of acceptance, then we will have the courage to change.

BLB

If any of you lacks wisdom, let him ask of God,
who gives to all liberally and without reproach,
and it will be given to him.   —JAMES 1:5

*W*ebster's Dictionary defines wisdom as "the quality of being wise; good judgment." The wisdom of the program guides us to make healthy decisions. It will take wisdom to recognize the games of manipulation we played in the past. Wisdom will lead us to set boundaries in relationships that would entrap us instead of setting us free. The wisdom of the program shines light in our darkness and illuminates for us a path toward freedom.

We can receive wisdom by listening to others who lived through the problems that we are now facing. We may not understand their advice from personal experience, but we can accept by faith the things we don't see clearly. This helps us continue in our spiritual process.

We also find wisdom by humbly asking God to provide it for us. God has promised to give liberally, generously, abundantly of his wisdom to anyone who will ask. This reminds us again to depend on God to guide us continually in our recovery.

Wisdom is the principal thing; therefore get wisdom. And in all your getting, get understanding (Prov 4:7).

CSH

Turn away my eyes from looking
at worthless things,
And revive me in Your way.
            —PS. 119:37

As we struggle with our addictions we need to ask ourselves, "What behavior do we need to change?" Jane's problem is her compulsive eating. She thinks that controlling her food daily is the only answer. She plans her meals, shops for just what she needs, packs her lunch, and has her snacks ready. She does everything perfectly. Then something comes along and disrupts her plans, and she feels out of control. Her child gets sick. Her husband comes home late for dinner. Her store does not carry the brand name she wants. She blames the failure of her diet on all the interruptions to her perfectly planned program.

Setting unrealistic goals leads to frustration. Needing things to be done perfectly creates more stress for us. Being a perfectionist sets us up for failure. As perfectionists, we expect too much of ourselves and others.

Learning to yield to more realistic expectations leads to a more balanced life.

                                                    BLB

He who heeds the word wisely will find good,
And whoever trusts in the LORD, happy is he.
                                        —PROV. 16:20

Happiness is a choice. You can act happy, talk happy and look happy. You can think happy thoughts. But often we choose to sit and mope.

Margaret pouts when things don't go her way. She could express her needs and ideas, or she could accept what others suggest. Instead of communicating, she uses negative, unhealthy behavior.

When we choose unhealthy behavior, we isolate ourselves from those who care about us. We say things to push them away, we are not pleasant to be with, and we also can influence them to be unhappy with us.

Barbara chooses healthy, positive behavior. The first thought she has every morning when she opens her eyes is *Lord, today I choose to be happy.* She says it brings her many rewards. She has a close relationship with her friends, better work conditions, less wear and tear on her nervous system, and a sense of humor in the little things. All of these are rewards for choosing happiness for the day.

————————

You can choose to be happy.

                                                        BLB

I perceive that to be with those I like is enough.
—WALT WHITMAN

Within each of us lies a longing to be loved, understood, and accepted by our families. Our hearts feel pain as we realize we may not experience the dream of a perfect family. Letting go of our fantasies moves us toward our recovery.

As we share with the people in our group, we realize how much we all have in common. We see that each of us has done things that we feel both ashamed of and embarrassed about. We can know all about each other and still feel love and acceptance. We come home to the program when we see that we are all alike. We need no longer fear rejection as we reach out to join a new family of caring people. We feel loved and know that we belong.

There is joy in learning that our real, healthy family is composed of people who love us, even if they are not our blood relatives. We spend time with people who want and need us. The program brims with folks who love and appreciate us if we only allow them to.

My heart gives thanks for the healing provided by loving friends who have now become my family.

CSH

If anyone among you thinks he is religious, and
does not bridle his tongue but deceives his own
heart, this one's religion is useless.
                                        —JAMES 1:26

As we list our strengths and weaknesses we need to
have a plan for change. If we are not careful, we will
feel bad about ourselves; then we will feel angry and
we'll take these angry feelings out on others or ourselves.

Joan repressed her anger. She took out her feelings
in the form of criticism, not only of others but of herself. She learned to encourage others and herself as
well. Martha had a hard time accepting other people's
differences. She learned to be more tolerant and accepting of others. Barbara learned to not think of herself as different from others, but as a unique child of
God. John is a talker. He is learning that 25 percent of
communication is talking, the other 75 percent is well
spent in listening.

These people have learned how to turn self-examination into self-fulfillment.

If you control your tongue, you have control over yourself.

                                                    BLB

Anger never motivates genuine change.
—DAVID HUMBERT

Many of us entered recovery with the problem of not knowing how to deal with our anger. We use words like *frustrated, aggravated,* or *hurt* to describe our feelings when we are actually angry. Some of us believe the lie that says if we love someone, then we can never show anger to them. Others are fearful that admitting anger would mean raging in the same way we saw our parents rage.

We all seem able to express anger toward ourselves. We practiced verbally abusing ourselves with thoughts that seem too cruel to repeat out loud. We remain unable to feel good about who we are if we constantly criticize ourselves.

Some of our behavior exposed dysfunction, but that does not make us bad. Anger with ourselves will keep us stuck in feelings of defeat. Gracious encouragement from others helps us make healthy changes in recovery. We can listen for negative thoughts and correct them with the gentle truth of our own preciousness.

I will be gracious to myself and meditate on the fact that I am a precious creation of God.

CSH

*Walk in the Spirit, and you shall not fulfill the lust
of the flesh. For the flesh lusts against the Spirit,
and the Spirit against the flesh; and these are
contrary to one another, so that you do not do
the things that you wish.*   —GAL. 5:16–17

It is hard to take a look in the mirror. Sure, we glance
in the mirror every once in awhile to check our tie or
see if our slip shows. We either like or dislike the image
we see. But do we see inside the person looking in the
mirror?

Let's glance in the mirror to check on our patience.
John prays for patience, but when he has a chance to
be patient, he forgets to call on the strength of the Lord
to help him achieve his prayer. Let's glance in the mirror to check on our anger. Barbara wears her feelings
on her shoulder. A slight bump and she reacts. Let's
glance in the mirror to check what we see in our eyes.
Do we see fear, guilt, or loneliness? It is hard work to
take our own inventory, but as we list strengths and
weaknesses we begin to see a picture of ourselves. We
can work on our weaknesses, one at a time, and add
them to our strengths list. We begin with the help of
our sponsor, and then we come before God and ask
him to remove our shortcomings.

Things do not change; we do (Henry David Thoreau).

BLB

Formula for failure: trying to please everyone.
—ANONYMOUS

During our childhood my brother and I caught a small lizard known as a chameleon. These little creatures intrigued us because they changed color. We delighted in their ability to turn brown and then change to bright green. They merely adapted to their environment in order to blend in safely.

Coming from a dysfunctional family can lead us to act like the chameleon. We adapt ourselves to whomever we happen to be with. We fear rejection or conflict, so we do not express our opinions. In fact, we are no longer certain what our opinions are. We expend lots of energy trying to blend in and stay safe. We try to gain acceptance through being agreeable at all times.

As we work through recovery we get in touch with our true self. Our improved self-esteem and God's power in our lives lead us to a place of being comfortable with who we are and how we feel. We no longer need to mimic other people.

Successful recovery is based on seeking to please God.

CSH

"Repent therefore and be converted, that your sins may be blotted out, so that times of refreshing may come from the presence of the Lord."

—ACTS 3:19

Alcoholism is a family disease. All members are affected by what alcohol does, not only the one who is the alcoholic.

Clara's husband is not an alcoholic, but he is a compulsive gambler. Jane's husband is a workaholic. Jack's wife compulsively shops and overspends their budget. Like alcoholism, these behaviors are unhealthy. They are also compulsive and can become addictive.

God wants us to lead a life that is healthy. He is there to support us and also to give us the strength and stability we need to stretch out for new behaviors.

Either stretch up to God or step back into his love. He is always there. We are the ones who need to move toward him.

BLB

*We can gain other people's approval if we do right
and try hard, but our own approval is worth a
hundred times more.* —MARK TWAIN

Harold used a lot of mental energy trying to figure out how other people might respond. He planned what to say, how to act, or where to go in order to gain the approval of others. At times he sought to manipulate and control the feelings of others by being overly nice. He felt a need to make sure everyone liked him.

This led Harold into patterns of stuffing needs and feelings. He was in touch with what other people felt, yet he didn't have a clue about his own needs and emotions. In therapy Harold learned to let go of controlling and allow each person to experience him in their own unique way. It felt new and uncomfortable at first, because it required changing old habits.

Many of us tried to perform in a way that gains the acceptance of others. We may have done so for such a long time that we feel uncertain about who we are. We need to spend more time learning about being our true selves and then give others the freedom to respond.

My life belongs to God and is not based on the approval of others.
CSH

I beseech you therefore, brethren, by the mercies of God, that you present your bodies a living sacrifice, holy, acceptable to God, which is your reasonable service.   —ROM. 12:1

Are you willing to turn your whole life over to God or do you want to just give him the part you are having problems with? Maybe your husband has a problem with alcohol. He comes home late for dinner, and you can tell he's been drinking. What part do you turn over to God, and what part of the problem do you handle yourself?

Perhaps you work hard all week, and on Sunday you want to sleep in. Things aren't going well at work. You are really irritable, because the other employees aren't doing their job the way you think they should. What part of this problem do you turn over to God, and what do you take care of yourself?

Your son has been staying out late and running with the wrong crowd. You are worried, so you stay up until he comes in and really yell at him. The next day you are so tired it is hard to concentrate at work. What part of this problem do you turn over to God?

God wants it all. He wants us to turn our hearts, our souls, our minds, and our power over to him.

God will be merciful as he prepares us for service to him.

BLB

> *"Blessed are the poor in spirit,*
> *For theirs is the kingdom of heaven."*
> —MATT. 5:3

Many of us play our game of life like Monopoly. We are intent on buying all we can buy, collecting all we can collect, and trying to stay out of jail. If we can throw a six, we'll land on Park Place and then we can buy it. If our partner lands on St. James, where we have a hotel, he will go bankrupt. Having just passed Go, we gain money to buy more.

Lawrence is down on his luck. He is poor in spirit. He uses alcohol and drugs to kill the pain. In his game of Monopoly, he goes directly to jail and pays the fine. He is poor in spirit, but where is the kingdom of heaven for him?

God's kingdom is within each of us, and it goes on through time and eternity. When we enter his kingdom we find real peace and power. We can recognize God's power if we respond to his love. We can own the world, collect the treasures of God's kingdom, and stay out of jail. We can pass Go and collect our rewards. For with the power in us, we are playing the game of life.

God is our power in the game of life.

BLB

*But one thing I do, forgetting those things which
are behind and reaching forward to those things
which are ahead . . .*   —PHIL. 3:13

Some of us look back to the past so often, we turn our
backs to the present and future. One of my friends continually reminds her husband of hurtful things he said
years ago, even though he asked her forgiveness.
These hurts cling to her mind like barnacles adhere to
the hull of a ship. Holding onto her anger has built a
barrier that blocks intimacy in the relationship and
keeps her feeling depressed.

Yes, we have a right to feel angry when we suffer
abuse. We need to grieve over the deep wounds in our
hearts. However, getting stuck in this process breeds
bitterness in our hearts and keeps us from reaching the
healing of forgiveness. We only move forward into a
healthy future when we stop looking backward.

Moving into the future will be scary because it requires taking risks and learning to trust again. God
teaches us how to forgive those who injured us in the
past. We draw on God for power in order to face the
new challenges and opportunities of the future.

Forgiveness is another word for letting go (Matthew Fox).

CSH

If it is possible, as much as depends on you, live peaceably with all men.   —ROM. 12:18

Anger and fear seem to be the only two emotions that we have when we begin recovery. The anger comes from years of repressed feelings toward people who have injured us. The injuries were physical, by being abused, or emotional, by being ignored or abandoned. In order to survive, we developed defenses to protect us from the pain of this abuse.

When Joanna came to see me, she was so angry that she could not even sit back in her chair. She perched on the edge, ready to spring forward to attack or to defend herself. As we talked through the situations where she felt such intense anger, we were able to uncover some other emotions. She saw that her behavior was often a reaction to someone else's behavior.

Joanna learned new, healthy behaviors in order to act rather than react in situations where she felt powerless. She learned to communicate her anger in a constructive way. She learned that fear was not trusting God. As she let go and let God have her fears, she uncovered feelings of trust, hope, and peace.

God can do for you what you cannot do for yourself.

BLB

Too many irons in the fire make the fire go out.
                    —JOHN W. WHITE

Many of us move toward activity. We volunteer for every committee, serve on every board, plan and attend every church function, and still put in more than forty hours each week on our regular job. We acknowledge that we aren't taking time for ourselves, but still we never slow down.

Have you ever stopped long enough to figure out what purpose the compulsion of drivenness serves for you? It looks so wonderful on the surface because you're such a servant and give your time so freely. However, God calls us to "be still and know that I am God" (Ps. 46:10).

Being still would mean you face your fears, your pain, and the anxiety that you continue to run from through the distraction of activities. You have two choices: either choose to slow down and face yourself or stop completely when you reach burnout.

God, give me the courage to slow down today so that I can get to know myself and you.

                                        CSH

Every wise woman builds her house,
But the foolish pulls it down with her hands.
                                        —PROV. 14:1

The need for others to approve of us destroys our inner peace. Approval needs to come from within ourselves.

Marilyn has spent her whole life trying to please others. First she tried to be the perfect daughter so that everyone would be happy. Then she tried to be the perfect wife so her husband would be happy. As a good neighbor she sought everyone else's approval about how she dressed, where her children went to school, how much volunteer work she did, and what kind of car she drove. As she got older, others depended on her to meet their needs. She had trained them to be that way so they would approve of her.

In recovery, Marilyn needed to recognize her own needs. Trying to please everyone else, fearing criticism if not performing perfectly, and ignoring her own needs were forms of manipulation on Marilyn's part. She found the solution in learning to rely on God's love and approval by living her life in his will. She learned to ask for what she needed, rather than manipulating others to get it.

Believe in yourself and others will believe in you also.

                                                        BLB

We humbly asked God to remove our shortcomings.

Some people are motivated by recognition, while others find security in being almost invisible. In a lot of cases these people marry each other. John and Mary are good examples. John was striving toward awards and career gains, and Mary was silently trying to hang on to every dime that came in. John needed clothes, cars, houses, and people, to feel comfortable. Mary just wanted to spend a quiet evening at home with the children. Both of them were dysfunctional because they depended on external means to provide their sense of well-being. If their needs were ignored, they became angry, and their anger became quite painful. They both found that reaching for a drink soothed the pain.

After recognizing their alcoholism, John and Mary found the way to recovery: They made an inventory of their behavior and were able to identify their personality characteristics and needs, became aware of their feelings, and finally asked God to remove their shortcomings.

Look in the mirror and see yourself as God sees you.

BLB

*Now faith is the substance of things hoped for, the
evidence of things not seen.*   —HEB. 11:1

Many of us place more faith in things than we do in
people. We believe a chair will hold us when we sit in it
or that an elevator will take us to our desired floor, but
we don't believe that people will remain dependable
when we need them. We often come to God as our
Higher Power with this same attitude.

Our logic tells us to demand proof. Faith requires accepting that God exists without being able to see him.
Our faith is a vital part of our recovery process. We
take one small step of faith at a time. With each step
forward, our trust begins to grow.

We learn to have faith by listening to others in recovery. They supply an unlimited number of miracles that
have occurred! We learn to trust that no matter what
happens to us, we can count on our Higher Power. We
rediscover what the founding members of the Twelve-
Step program learned as we see how far other members have grown in recovery. God is able to do for us
what we are unable to do for ourselves.

Today I will ask God to deepen my faith and trust in his ability.
                                                        CSH

If any of you lacks wisdom, let him ask of God,
who gives to all liberally and without reproach.
—JAMES 1:5

When we pray the Serenity Prayer and ask for acceptance, what are we struggling to accept? Is it the behavior of our spouse? Do we feel criticized when what we need is love and affirmation? Why do we feel a lack of peace and serenity?

Let's say you have had a busy day with the housework, three preschoolers, and errands to run, and your spouse comes in tired and ready for dinner. Do you both take time to greet each other with a smile, a hug, and a warm hello, or are you only concerned with yourselves?

If we give love and praise to others who struggle with their problems, then our problems won't grow so big by our constant dwelling on them. Our hearts may feel empty without words of praise from others, but when we treat others as we would like to be treated, we receive a gift in return. We need wisdom to know how to change.

_____

God, grant me the serenity to accept the things I cannot change, the courage to change the things I can, and the wisdom to know the difference (Reinhold Niebuhr).

BLB

And whatever you do in word or deed, do all in the name of the Lord Jesus.   —COL. 3:17

During the Korean conflict several soldiers had a young Korean houseboy. They played endless jokes on him, such as nailing his shoes to the floor and setting water above doorways to fall on him. At Christmas the soldiers felt guilty and decided to stop the practical jokes. They explained to the houseboy that there would be no more nailed-down shoes and no more water poured on him. He responded that he would "no more spit in soup."

We all despise injustice, and we hate the thought of being ripped off or overlooked, especially at our jobs. Many of us find a passive way to get even by "spitting in the soup." We may leave work early or call in sick when we feel fine. This passive-aggressive way of expressing our anger does not solve the problem. God has a healthy plan for us in unfair situations. He wants us to take the focus off what those around us aren't giving us and turn our eyes toward him.

We can detach from other people and decide to do our work as an honor to God. It makes our burden much lighter when we focus on pleasing God and not on pleasing people.

CSH

"But seek first the kingdom of God."
—MATT. 6:33

When I was in high school I can remember arguing that what I was doing in math class couldn't possibly have any relevance to what I wanted to do when I grew up. Having to write papers for English class had nothing to do with the way I saw my life after school.

The first twenty years of my life in school centered on the struggle to learn. I thought I knew everything I needed for life. The second twenty years was a very humbling experience. The humility came from seeing what I did not know.

They didn't teach courses in marriage and family, parenting, behavior modification, and communication when I went to school. I learned by doing, and what I did was not always given a good or even a passing grade. However, the hope of future generations rests in the fact that we do the best we can. With God's help we can move forward by sharing with our children how to make healthier choices in life.

Turn the past over to God. Then meet him each morning to gain knowledge for living one day at a time.

BLB

Humility is not thinking less of yourself, but
thinking of yourself less.   —ANONYMOUS

The program contains a recurrent theme of developing humility. In our past, we were prideful in thinking that we could handle our addictions alone. Humility means that we learn to let go of our pride and admit that we need help from our Higher Power. Being humble requires us to be teachable and to surrender our will to God. We stop trying to be in control, because we realize that our control never worked.

Humility brings joy and helps us battle against the cunning, powerful dependencies in our lives. Truly humble people receive a great amount of wisdom and strength from God. Through humility we gain a greater sense of hope, trust, faith, love, and forgiveness. Humility gives us the ability to listen to others and care for their needs and feelings.

We need to get rid of our misconceptions about what humility means. Humility has nothing to do with meekness or putting ourselves down. It means that we face the fact that we need a proper relationship with God.

———————————

When we submit to God's leadership, we don't even have to try to be humble. It just comes naturally.

CSH

For everyone who asks receives, and he who seeks
finds, and to him who knocks it will be opened.
—MATT. 7:8

As we work through the Twelve-Step program we learn to admit we need God's power in our life if we are going to live in a healthy way. We cannot give up our addictive, compulsive behavior without his help and without our being willing to turn our lives over to him.

With God's help we looked at our past relationships, family, and childhood, and we made a list of things about ourselves that we need to change. Maybe one of them was to listen more and talk less. What difference has the power of God made in this area of your life? Another area may be to be more considerate of others. Has God helped make a difference here? What about the one where you want to fix everybody else? When we give the job to God, it is amazing what a better job he does than we could have done.

These changes come slowly, but the results bring many blessings in our life. As we learn to listen more, friends and family seem to be more drawn to us in an open, trustful way. As we reach out to others, our relationships become more meaningful.

God has a plan. He just needs us to look to him, do his will, and not expect him to compliment us on doing his job for him.

BLB

> *I will guide you with My eye.*
> *Do not be like the horse or like the mule . . .*
> *Which must be harnessed with bit and bridle.*
> —PS. 32:8–9

When I was young I enjoyed riding horses. The only thing I disliked was putting the bit in the horse's mouth because it seemed cruel. My father explained that horses are large, high-spirited animals who require a bit and bridle for control.

There were many times when my horse, Beauty, was in a docile mood and allowed me to guide her with verbal commands. It pleased me when riding seemed so effortless and relaxed. Other times were difficult when Beauty had no desire to be ridden, and I had to pull firmly on the reins to keep her under control.

None of us wishes God to "bridle" us, and that will not be necessary if we come to him in humble dependence on his power to help us change. We need to seek his will for our lives and obediently follow his direction by trusting him in every situation. God wants to lead us gently, so let's humbly submit to his guidance.

I will submit to being guided by God's gentle, loving leadership.

CSH

I sought the LORD, and He heard me,
And delivered me from all my fears.
                                        —PS. 34:4

Anna really struggled with expressing her anger in a constructive way. She continually let men be verbally abusive to her. It was not clear to her that she was being abused, though she felt intense hurt and rejection. Instead of seeing their behavior as abuse, she thought she had done something wrong. Her way of reacting was either to get angry and start an argument or to repress her feelings and then become depressed.

We worked together practicing what she was going to do to change her behavior. It was not long before she had an opportunity to try it out. Joe called her and during the conversation told her he had invited someone else to the Christmas dance. She felt angry, betrayed, and hurt. But without raging or repressing, she told him what she was thinking and feeling.

She called me the next morning to share what had happened. As we went over the conversation, I affirmed her behavior.

Trying to change our behavior can be frightening and overwhelming at times, but humbly asking God to remove our shortcomings is a beginning for change.

Affirmations encourage and support your growth. Affirm yourself on a daily basis.

                                                    BLB

Humility is our acceptance of ourselves.
—ANONYMOUS

Terri had trouble understanding what humility means. She remembered feeling humiliated and embarrassed when she tripped and fell down at her high school prom. Terri imagined that having true humility involved keeping a negative image of herself. While working Step Seven, she learned the true meaning of humility.

God does not desire to shame us in this process of being humble. He desires that we learn to submit ourselves to his will for us. Humility means that we admit that we cannot remove our shortcomings by using our own willpower. Humility also means that we admit that our character defects have damaged us and others. One of the problems of our addiction was denying the amount of pain it caused.

As we start to realize the severity of the damage we caused, we see that we are helpless in changing ourselves. We can then surrender to God and allow him to take a place of leadership in our lives. Only God has the power to rebuild broken lives.

When I submit to God, he can put the pieces of my broken life back together.

CSH

> *Therefore humble yourselves under the mighty*
> *hand of God, that He may exalt you in due time,*
> *casting all your care upon Him, for He cares*
> *for you.*
>   —1 PETER 5:6–7

One summer we had planned a two-week vacation. Because of a conflict in scheduling the vacation home we were going to use, I almost canceled the trip. I found out that we were only going to have the cabin for one week instead of two, because another couple wanted to use it right after us. If I had canceled the trip because I could not have my way, I would have missed one of the most memorable family vacations ever. I could not have changed to be more accepting without asking for strength from the Lord. I couldn't take disappointments very well, but after I took my shortcomings to the Lord, he gave me the courage to become more accepting of disappointments in life.

Only by being honest about our own behavior are we able to drop the masks and disguises we use to keep from seeing things as they really are. We need this humility in order to ask for help from the Lord.

God, grant us the courage to be more accepting of life's difficulties.
         BLB

Who can understand his errors?
Cleanse me from secret faults.
—PS. 19:12

We seldom want to admit that we have secret sins. We act like the little boy who hated to take a bath. He especially disliked it when his mother used soap and a washcloth to clean those hard-to-get spots on his face. During one episode, the mother tried to reason with him and asked, "Don't you want to be clean?" "Yes," he responded, "but couldn't you just dust my face?"

As with all of our defects of character, the hidden areas need to be cleansed. In recovery we often want to experience an occasional dusting by going to group meetings and admitting our obvious shortcomings. God desires for us to learn the daily discipline of allowing him to show us areas that need to be cleansed. As we spend time in God's Word the light of his truth becomes brighter, and we can more clearly see the flaws in our hearts.

Each of us needs to humbly ask God to reveal the secret sins that we have locked away.

A superficial dusting will not clean out the root of the problem.

CSH

> *So it was, that while they were there, the days were*
> *completed for her to be delivered. . . . And behold,*
> *an angel of the Lord stood before them, and the*
> *glory of the Lord shone around them. . . . And*
> *suddenly there was with the angel a multitude of*
> *the heavenly host praising God.*
>
> —LUKE 2:6–13

When children are born, the parents usually send out birth announcements. God made his announcement a little differently. He sent out his announcements to the world before his Son was even born. He even sent angels to Mary and Joseph to tell them that they would have a son. Then he had the angel tell them that the baby was to be named Jesus. When the baby was born, his parents did not have to send out announcements. God's angels in heaven sang the announcement of his birth and told all to come worship the newborn baby.

When we come to Step Seven and prepare to ask Jesus to remove our shortcomings, let us think back to the promise, the announcement, the birth, and the death of God's Son. Jesus came and died for our sins so that we can be forgiven. We should ask for forgiveness with great humility and accept that someone's life has been sacrificed that we may live in peace.

Let us go out and witness what the Lord has done for us as a new birth takes place in us.

BLB

For God has not given us a spirit of fear, but of power and of love and of a sound mind.
—2 TIM. 1:7

Fear played a major role in many of our lives. We fear intimacy, God, the past, change, and ourselves. Working Step Seven may feel like a frightening part of recovery. Although we desire God to remove our shortcomings, we're not sure what will be left of us.

We can rest assured that God does not desire to damage us. He only wants to remove those traits that harm us and stop us from being ourselves. We each maintain our personalities and the mannerisms that make us special individuals.

God will take away many of our negative traits. Some of the self-defeating traits will change to the positive aspect of the same trait. For instance, determination is the healthy part of obsessiveness.

God desires for us not to fear Step Seven, but to trust that he only removes the traits that keep us from becoming like him.

God desires to conform us to his image, and that requires removing our negative traits and behaviors.

CSH

He who despises his neighbor sins;
But he who has mercy on the poor,
*   happy is he.*   —PROV. 14:21

Today's world is so fast and so busy that we can go for weeks without being alone with a friend. Many of us do this to avoid intimacy. But giving to friends is a way of tapping into an energy source. Think about that gift you bought for a friend. Remember that after you found it, wrapped it, and presented it to him, you got more joy out of his surprise than he did out of receiving the gift. This is energy received from giving of your time to others—to walk with them, talk with them, listen to their needs, and share your interest in them. This is what Jesus told us friendship was all about.

In the hymn "I Come to the Garden Alone," we sing about how Jesus walks and talks with us. He did this to show us how to humble ourselves to be available to others in need. God helps us lay aside our self-centered need to use people for our comfort. We open a door to let in the happiness received by sharing our life with others.

_____

George Bernard Shaw said, "The surest way to be miserable is to have the leisure to wonder whether or not you are happy." Happiness usually comes when we are giving to others.

BLB

*Recognizing that something needs to be changed is
the first step toward changing it.*
—DONNA TILLINGHAST

One of the reasons that God does not allow us to change instantly is because we would not learn anything. Things that come to us easily seem to not hold much value. Recovery makes a lasting impression when we put forth effort and hard work to bring about change.

The journey of recovery involves walking, stumbling, sometimes falling down, getting up, and continuing to move forward. Fortunately we do not have to walk through this process alone. God promises to provide us with the wisdom and strength we need when we are willing to be humble and ask for his guidance. We can also get encouragement from other people who have experienced the journey. The insight and support they provide for us offers a great blessing.

Instead of feeling frustrated when we recognize a defect in our behavior, we should be encouraged that we are gaining insight and moving forward in our recovery.

God will not magically remove our shortcomings, but he will supply all our needs.

CSH

I sought the LORD, and He heard me,
And delivered me from all my fears.
—PS. 34:4

One characteristic of people who grew up in dysfunctional families is that they blame other people for their problems. They usually get into recovery when they have to take a look at themselves.

Alcoholism is a family disease that spreads from generation to generation. So do other obsessive/addictive behavior patterns. Your father may have been an alcoholic, and you said you would never drink. Today, however, you spend all your time working—you are a workaholic. Maybe you compulsively shop, overeat, or gamble. These are behaviors that have been learned and can be changed.

When we seek the Lord, he will help us remove these obsessive/addictive behavior patterns. We can start by attending Twelve-Step meetings. Alcoholics Anonymous is for the compulsive drinker. Overeaters Anonymous, Narcotics Anonymous, and many other groups provide support and friends with similar experiences to yours. Many churches now offer Twelve-Step programs for Christian living.

Begin today to break the unhealthy cycle of behavior from past generations by seeking the Lord in all that you do.

BLB

The LORD is near to all who call upon Him.
—PS. 145:18

When I first asked God to remove my shortcomings, I wanted him to perform a quick surgical procedure on my emotions. It took some time for me to understand that working Step Seven would not produce instant change. It simply set the process in motion.

Gradually, through time and practice, I learned to stop trying so hard and to surrender to God. I realized that I wasn't helping people by taking care of them. I kept them from growing and I ignored my own needs.

Each of us must learn to let go of other people. Letting go does not mean that our desire to caretake, control, or manipulate will never come back. It means that we learn to stay alert and be aware of our own motives and needs.

As we grow we need to develop a sense of gentle compassion for ourselves and others. We are all human and are allowed to make mistakes. We don't need to criticize ourselves when we seem slow to change. Our major goal is acceptance and a healthy love of ourselves and others.

The more we accept ourselves, the more we move toward healing.
                                                                CSH

*And my God shall supply all your need according
to His riches in glory by Christ Jesus.*
                                    —PHIL. 4:19

We may have a fear of abandonment that began during our childhood. Maybe we felt unwanted or unloved as a child because our need for love was not met. Over a period of time we came to resent those who did not meet our needs.

Judy has had four serious love relationships in the past sixteen years. She weighs each man on how much he can give to her, be there for her, and fill her needs. But when he asks for something in return from her, she runs to the safety of isolation.

When Judy was a child her parents overprotected her; they did not prepare her to be alone. Her anger at her parents' control has turned to resentment of anyone who fails to meet her needs. She fears that if she lets go of a relationship, even if it is a bad one, she will be left all alone. She is very angry that she cannot make others be there for her whenever she needs them. Through Christian counseling Judy has learned that letting go of her resentment leaves her open for loving relationships.

---

*Letting go and giving up our fears to God insures us that he will fill
that empty space of loneliness with love and peace.*

                                                    BLB

Our patience will achieve more than our force.
—EDMUND BURKE

At the age of thirty Matthew was climbing the corporate ladder. He had never played golf before, but he felt that it would be in his best interest to learn so he could interact better with his business associates.

Matthew bought a set of golf clubs and took private lessons. He soon learned that golf was difficult and frustrating. His shoulders ached from practicing his swing, and he often developed painful blisters on his hands from gripping the golf club. Several times he felt angry about his lack of progress and wanted to give up. His instructor encouraged Matthew. He told him he had the potential to be a good golfer, but he needed patience with himself and diligence in practicing.

Change requires practice and, like learning a golf swing, it will sometimes be frustrating. Our best approach is to be gentle with ourselves during the process and allow others to instruct us.

If at first you don't succeed, try, try again.

CSH

Jesus . . . spoke to them, saying, "All authority has been given to Me in heaven and on earth. . . . and lo, I am with you always, even to the end of the age."
—MATT. 28:18–20

Were there times when you felt lonely as a child? Maybe your best friend was out of town and you didn't have anyone to play with. Perhaps your parents went out and you were alone in the house. When I was a child and was disciplined for something I did wrong, I was sent to my room "to think about" what I had done. I felt alone and rejected. All I could think about was myself and how I was feeling, not about what I had done.

Now that I am an adult I find that there are still times when I need to go to my room and think about what I have done. Maybe I hurt someone's feelings by being unkind or impatient. Maybe I told a lie. Maybe I rejected God's love for me by putting myself down. Whatever the reason, I still find myself going to my room to think about my actions. As a child I felt alone in this room, but today I know that God is there with me. He forgives me and encourages me to love him, others, and myself, because he sent his Son to die for my sins.

We ask for wisdom to know that God is always there, even when we have sinned.

BLB

As far as the east is from the west,
So far has He removed our transgressions from us.
—PS. 103:12

If you began a journey to the east and planned to circle around the globe by heading west, it would be an endless trip. You would just keep going west, never reaching east. That is how far God has removed our transgressions from us! God must really care about us a lot to relieve us so completely no matter what we have done and what our weaknesses are. God really loves us the way we are, but he loves us too much to leave us this way. He keeps on refining us, teaching us, forgiving us, and loving us.

It doesn't matter if you have wallowed in the same shortcomings for many years; it's never too late to have a heart-to-heart talk with yourself and God about these things. It brings an amazing clarity and peace to talk to God about your pain, desires, and even your dreams. It also helps you come to terms with your own strengths and weaknesses. It's like looking in a three-way mirror and seeing views of yourself that you haven't seen before. God continually works with us. He makes subtle refinements, masterfully shaping us in his image.

—————

The Lord cares about us so much that he completely forgives our sins.

FLM

Humble yourselves in the sight of the Lord, and He will lift you up.
                                        —JAMES 4:10

In Step Seven we ask God to remove defects from us such as unresolved grief and anger, self-destructive behaviors, controlling behavior, and dependency. These problems rob us of joy and keep us from having a healthy relationship with God, ourselves, or others.

We are not required to force ourselves to change. Numerous attempts at change failed for us in the past. God simply asks that we have a heart full of humility and willingness to change.

Humility means that we accept our powerlessness to remove these defects of character. Humility also requires seeing that we are not all-powerful but that God certainly is. He has the ability to "create in [us] a clean heart . . . and renew a steadfast spirit within [us]" (Ps. 51:10). Creating a clean heart takes time, but as we humble ourselves God remains faithful to complete the process and lift us up.

God has the power to remove the heavy burdens that have weighed down our hearts.

                                                    CSH

Put on the whole armor of God, that you may be able to stand against the wiles of the devil. For we do not wrestle against flesh and blood, but . . . against the rulers of the darkness of this age, against spiritual hosts of wickedness in the heavenly places.   —EPH. 6:11–12

Charles has a tremendous ability to solve problems. He is quick to see the whole picture, he takes the time to analyze the situation, and then he formulates a plan for solving the problem. Jane prefers to hit the problem head-on and watch the sparks fly. Charles just jokes when Jane faces a really difficult problem. In reality though, he wishes she would slow down, take her time, and solve problems like he does. Of course, she wishes he would not spend so much time presenting her with the solution to her problems. She sometimes tries to solve her problems before he tells her what to do.

Humbly asking God to remove our shortcomings helps us work together to solve problems.

As we list areas of our life that are currently sources of concern, pain, resentment, or sadness, awareness of what can be changed gives us a sense of peace and serenity.

BLB

I sought the LORD, and He heard me,
And delivered me from all my fears.
　　　　　　　—PS. 34:4

A lot of things in our lives today pull us down, like television, movies, and bars. Have you ever felt so low that you thought God didn't care about you and wasn't listening to your prayers? You might have been thinking like Sharon. She felt that she was not worthy of God's blessings and that he had done all he was going to do for her. Sharon just did not know how to make things better.

If you feel low and in despair, do the one thing that you probably want to do least: pray! Yes, you've tried it before in many ways; pleading, bargaining, discussing, reasoning, threatening, standing, and kneeling. God loves for us to talk with him, no matter what mood we're in and no matter what is on our minds. We're his children, and he wants us to be open and share our feelings, joys, and fears. He is always there to listen, and his love is unconditional. Just think of your own children. Aren't you committed to them no matter what their moods or actions are?

―――――――――

The Lord honors our prayers and knows our hearts.

FLM

*All changes, even the most longed for, have [some
sadness]; for what we leave behind us is a part of
ourselves; we must die to one life before we can
enter into another!*   —ANATOLE FRANCE

Asking God to remove his dependencies felt frightening to Winston. He felt a little out of control and was uncertain how God would change him. Winston wondered if his friends would recognize him or if he needed to aim for perfection from now on.

Through his support group, Winston learned that healthy change involves a slow process of emotional and spiritual healing. He experienced pain at times, but he soon learned to welcome his pain. He knew it led him past his frozen emotions and taught him to get in touch with his genuine feelings. The hurts of Winston's past were only able to heal once he felt the pain he had buried inside.

Through our years of recovery we will continue to change. We are not responsible for changing ourselves, but we must allow God to bring about changes. He does this by making us aware of areas that are unhealthy.

I will trust God even in the areas that are most personal to me.

CSH

If we confess our sins, He is faithful and just to
forgive us our sins and to cleanse us from all
unrighteousness.
            —1 JOHN 1:9

A couple who was going through the Twelve-Step program struggled with taking each other's inventory. She would remind him of the things he needed to change and he would list her faults. Many of us are like them. We should remember that we make people angry when we try to take their inventory.

Thank goodness God is more gentle with us than we are with each other. He helps us to see the easy things to change first so that we can build up our confidence. Then he guides us through the more difficult problems.

Sometimes we ask God to take away a bad habit and it doesn't seem to go away. Then we need to work harder on our willingness to turn our life over to God.

Prayer is the way we confess to God our shortcomings and ask him to change us.

            BLB

*God willed to make known what are the riches
of the glory . . . which is Christ in you, the hope
of glory.*   —COL. 1:27

As children we wished on a lucky star and tossed
coins into a wishing well. Some of us never outgrew
these childish whims. We assume that if we wait long
enough and behave well enough, something magical
will keep us from having to face the trials of today.

It doesn't work! Instead, the pain festers and the trials escalate. When our bubble of false hope finally
bursts, we are left shattered with problems that must
be dealt with. We find ourselves overwhelmed.

Asking God to remove our shortcomings is one step
in dealing with that festering backlog. With the help of
his grace and other recovering friends, we face the hidden monsters of the past. We learn that we are no
longer helpless children battered by the choices of
other people. We can make our own choices, and these
choices can improve our world. We give up the hope of
a future utopia and learn to bask in the pleasures of
today's sunshine.

Wishing will not change us, but working the program will.

CSH

*Now this is the confidence that we have in Him,
that if we ask anything according to His will, He
hears us. And if we know that He hears us,
whatever we ask, we know that we have the
petitions that we have asked of Him.*

—1 JOHN 5:14–15

In a healthy family, touching brings comfort and shows love. Healthy parents hold and touch their children when they cry; the children then learn that they can receive comfort from others by touching.

Carolyn grew up in an abusive family where touching left painful memories. As a child she was touched in an abusive way by someone who hit, slapped, and hurt her in physical and sexual ways. She fears being touched today, even though it is also painful not being touched at all.

To heal, persons who have been hurt need to turn to someone who can help them learn the positive comfort of healthy touching and ask the Lord to heal the pain. Whatever we ask he hears, and we are comforted by knowing that we have what we ask of him.

God can heal memories and open the way to a trusting relationship with others.

BLB

Sometimes we must turn away in order to return to God in dignity. —LINDA KRASIENKO

To some of us God seems critical, watchful, suspicious, judgmental, or even demanding. Who would willingly submit to such a brute? We need a new perspective of God. We need to focus on his mercy, his grace, his forgiveness, and his love.

This task is difficult for those who never knew loving authority figures. We may need to start by seeing God through the eyes of a Christian friend or therapist. Many of us will need to process our anger toward the adults who left us with such a harsh view of God.

In some cases, we have to pull away from God in order to determine which of our mental images came from parents and church and which were the truth from the life of Christ himself. This task may be long, lonely, tedious, and painful. For a time we may feel we have no God at all. However, the God we can learn to know is trustworthy, loving, and one to whom we can confidently submit.

Our vision of God may be distorted from the past, but we can learn to rest in the truth of his abundant love for us.

CSH

Let brotherly love continue.
—HEB. 13:1

We sometimes get so caught up in our own problems that we build a wall around ourselves. As we begin to recover from isolation, we need to step out of our rut. If we have been withdrawing from people in anger, we need to take a step toward them in kindness. The behavior they use to hurt us comes from their pain. As we stop *reacting* to them, we are free to *act* toward others in a spirit of love and kindness.

A man I know lashes out at others whenever he feels a loss of control over his own life. He puts his wife down, speaks sarcastically to others, and gets angry at other drivers on the street. When he behaves in this negative way, he is asking for assurance that he is okay.

Reacting to another's negative behavior only adds fuel to the fire. Choosing kind words and acting in a helpful way can extinguish the fire. After a violent verbal outburst we are left with a feeling of complete exhaustion. When we break this cycle by changing our behavior, we are left with a feeling of peace.

Let today be a happy day, full of kind words and helpful deeds.

BLB

We made a list of all persons we had harmed and became willing to make amends to them all.

The Ten Commandments have a lot of relevance to each of us in our daily lives. They're not just for murderers and thieves. They're for all of us, and they are easily violated in many different ways. You can kill people in more ways than one. You can ruin their reputation or gossip about them.

Imagine throwing a handful of confetti into the air on a windy day and then trying to recover it all. That's how impossible it is to take back words spoken in jealousy, hatred, lust, or lies. Harsh words are like daggers that tear the flesh.

Are your family members and friends wearing bandages right now? Don't hurt others whom Christ died to help. Use your tongue to help people feel better. Love manifests itself in encouraging others, not in tearing them apart.

Loving others means not hurting them in any way.

FLM

Your word is a lamp to my feet
And a light to my path.
        —PS. 119:105

During my childhood I spent several weeks each summer at a camp nestled deep in the pines of Mississippi. Every Wednesday night we hiked a mile down a gravel road to a creepy place called Hangman's Bridge. When we reached the bridge, we sat and heard ghost stories.

Trees covered the road in many places, and if there was no moon out, it was difficult to see your hand in front of your face. Only a few counselors carried flashlights. You can imagine 150 eleven year olds marching down a road at 10:00 P.M. with only five or six lights shining. Needless to say, I always managed to walk strategically close to a counselor with a flashlight, and even then I was often still afraid.

Beginning to recognize the people we have harmed can feel like walking through a scary place in the dark. We have never prepared to make amends before, and the changes ahead of us feel uncertain and frightening. In the same way I clung to the counselor with the flashlight, we each need someone to shine a light so we can see the way to go. God tells us that his Word provides light for our path.

We can study God's Word in order to gain direction and be illuminated to the truth found there.

                                            CSH

"Then his master . . . said to him, 'You wicked servant! I forgave you all that debt because you begged me. Should you not also have had compassion on your fellow servant, just as I had pity on you?'"   —MATT. 18:32–33

When we reach Step Eight, we make a list of the people we have harmed. Jennifer began her list of names and noticed she felt uncomfortable when she wrote Jeff's name. She realized the hardest part of her recovery was being willing to ask for Jeff's forgiveness. Half the battle was won just by putting his name on her list. At least she was admitting that she had done some harm to him and was willing to face up to it. The anger that she felt was the wall that kept them separated in their relationship.

Our feelings tell us when there is something there that needs to be resolved. It is called our conscience. When we add a name to our inventory and get an uncomfortable feeling, we need to examine that relationship. We need to search our conscience to see what harm was done by us and then make amends to the other person.

We must be willing to admit our responsibility in relationships and make amends to those we have harmed.

BLB

> *"You shall know the truth, and the truth shall make you free."*
> —JOHN 8:32

Wayne entered therapy with the problem of dividing reality into all-or-nothing, black-or-white extremes. This form of thinking led him to miss the more balanced "grey areas" of life. Wayne demanded perfection of himself and others. This extreme expectation set him up for a lot of frustration. As he worked Step Eight he became aware of the unfair standard he had set for himself and others, and he worked to change his thinking to a more truthful version.

The issues where we get confused about the grey areas are more personal. As students, many of us believed that anything other than an A in class meant failure. When we believe that we can never do anything right, it produces extreme thinking. The truth is that all of us have areas where we perform above average, average, and below average. We each have different capabilities in different areas. That doesn't make us good or bad; it makes us individuals.

God tells us that knowing the truth gives us freedom. Usually the truth about ourselves is in the middle, grey area. We need to seek the freedom of having balanced thinking.

Have a truth check. Do the things you believe about yourself produce freedom?

CSH

*Therefore judge nothing before the time, until the
Lord comes, who will both bring to light the hidden
things of darkness and reveal the counsels of the
hearts; and then each one's praise will come
from God.*   —1 COR. 4:5

God knows that we are in the process of growing,
dealing with tough issues, and sincerely battling our
sinful natures. He has all the facts. He knows our hearts
and motivations; he is always a fair and forgiving
judge. Sometimes we can't resist judging our own
actions and thoughts. Part of this may be the perfectionism that lies deep inside us. As we come to know
the Savior and know that he's perfect, we seem to expect this of ourselves. When we do something sinful or
stupid, it's only human nature to try to cover our tracks
so others don't find out. Still, we can't hide it from ourselves, and God knows about it because he is omni-
scient.

We can be comforted to know that God will judge us
fairly because he knows our hearts.

God knows and understands the hearts of his children.

FLM

> *Be anxious for nothing, but in everything by*
> *prayer and supplication, with thanksgiving, let your*
> *requests be made known to God; and the peace of*
> *God, which surpasses all understanding, will guard*
> *your hearts and minds through Christ Jesus.*
> —PHIL. 4:6–7

Worrying is an act that seems as natural as breathing to some of us. If things in life are going too smoothly, we worry because we don't have anything to worry about! Most of the things we worry about are out of our control. We waste our time worrying that we should have done things differently in the past.

We can come before God in specific prayer, stating in plain words the hurts and needs of our heart. We can really open up and talk with God. He will never reject us or think that we are foolish. He has promised to give us peace in our hearts when we turn our problems over to him.

Many of us worry about making amends and how people will respond to us. God offers prayer as a formula for easing our worried hearts.

Prayer comforts our hearts and reminds us that God has total control.

CSH

*Let each of you look out not only for his own
interests, but also for the interests of others.*
                              —PHIL. 2:4

Jane had a friend, Carol, who had been very important to her. After Jane married and had children, she
did not have time for Carol. About fifteen years later,
Jane got a call that her friend was in the hospital dying
of cancer. Jane went to see her and continued to see
her as much as she could until she died. Jane's feelings
of sadness were not only over Carol's death but also
over the loss of their friendship and time together.

Many of our relationships from the past are no
longer important to us today. What happened? Did we
forget about how important they were to us? Did we
hurt them by our actions? Sometimes we just let people
slip out of our lives by not having time for them.

The hardest part about Step Eight is having to admit
that we have harmed someone by our actions. As you
record names on your relationship inventory, names of
people who were important to you in the past, note
how important they are to you today.

---

*Relationships cannot grow if they are ignored. Treat them like fine
jewels that are to be maintained and treasured.*

                                              BLB

> *Therefore you are inexcusable, O man, whoever*
> *you are who judge, for in whatever you judge*
> *another you condemn yourself; for you who*
> *judge practice the same things.*   —ROM. 2:1

A bumper sticker says, "Christians aren't perfect . . . just forgiven." That's true—so why do we expect perfection from our mates, relatives, co-workers, church members, and pastors?

It's clear in Scripture that we are not supposed to judge other people and speculate whether they are sinful or righteous. When we do, we are trying to take the Lord's place. No matter how hard we try, probably not a day goes by that we don't judge ourselves or others. We condemn someone if they drink on Saturday night or watch a questionable movie, but we ignore our own sins of gossiping or stretching the truth. We use the standards set by our church groups or neighborhood instead of using God's standards.

Every time you catch yourself judging or slandering someone else, stop and think that you may be committing the same sins.

God alone is in control, and he alone is our judge.

FLM

Hope and patience are two sovereign remedies for all, the surest reposals, the softest cushions to lean on in adversity.   —ROBERT BURTON

Have you ever watched a child learning to walk? Friends and relatives get excited and bring out their movie cameras. They coax the child forward by holding out a favorite toy and cooing words of encouragement. Cheers accompany each attempted step.

Learning includes some painful falls, yet it never occurs to a child to stop trying to walk. Babies have not learned to fear defeat. They move forward in their attempts and eventually learn to walk.

Making amends takes time. Frustration overwhelms us when we set unrealistic expectations for how quickly we "should" work Step Eight. We would never expect a child to walk in one day, so we should not expect to rush ourselves through recovery. We need to graciously encourage ourselves by how far we have come instead of focusing on how far we have left to go.

Let us have hope for our future and patience with our present.

CSH

> *Love suffers long and is kind; love does not envy;*
> *love does not parade itself, is not puffed up; . . .*
> *thinks no evil; does not rejoice in iniquity, but*
> *rejoices in the truth.*   —1 COR. 13:4–6

John and Virginia had known Jack and Gloria since early marriage. They had raised their children together, laughed together, cried together, and looked forward to spending time together as they grew old. An incident ruined that friendship. Both couples were at fault, but each couple still blames the other.

When Jack and Gloria moved to another state, they left their dog with John and Virginia. The dog became too much for John and Virginia to handle, so they gave the dog to some other friends. A year later Jack and Gloria moved back and came to claim their dog. They were very hurt that the dog was gone. Even though they said they understood, they drop little reminders to this day about how their dog was given away. Resentment has built up on both sides and has affected the friendship.

Apologizing and forgiving is the easy part. Letting go of the feelings is difficult.

BLB

*The prayer of amends must be a way of life, not
just a sad cry at the end of failure.*
—ANONYMOUS

Alonzo saw Nan for the first time in four years when
they met for lunch. He had planned for months to
make amends with her for his act of adultery during
their marriage. Alonzo was truly sorry for the wreck-
age caused by his actions.

Nan refused to accept his apology because she still
carried deep anger toward her ex-husband. All Alonzo
could do was tell her how bad he felt for causing her
pain.

We offer amends with the hope of healing relationships. We can only pray that, in time, God will use our
request for forgiveness to soften the hearts of those we
have harmed. Our recovery requires our willingness to
offer amends. Some of our past mistakes cannot be
corrected with an apology.

God can use our willingness to help in the future healing of others.
CSH

"And just as you want men to do to you, you also do to them likewise."
           —LUKE 6:31

John is thirty-two years old. He has had trouble completing his college credits for graduation, trouble holding a job, and repeated trouble in close personal relationships. John blames his father for the repeated failures in his life. John's father is an alcoholic.

Jane is twenty-eight years old. An accountant, Jane is overweight and very resentful of her mother's interference in her life. She blames her lack of a close personal relationship and her weight on her mother. Jane is the daughter of an alcoholic.

Both John and Jane are in recovery in an Adult Children of Alcoholics Twelve-Step program. John is learning to accept God as a loving father who accepts him as he is. He is starting to call upon God for strength and the power to fulfill his goals in life. Jane is beginning to see God as loving and caring. She is realizing that her body is a temple for the Holy Spirit. She is able to value herself and take care of herself in a more healthy way one day at a time.

Our personal progress in recovery is directly related to our acceptance of the past and our ability to change our behavior toward ourselves and others.

BLB

> *To err is human, to forgive divine.*
> —ALEXANDER POPE

Whenever Monica makes a mistake, she pulls up a mental list of all her past failures. She starts to go over all of her dependent relationships from the past, and criticizes herself for the "stupid" things she did. She believes that if she mentally punishes herself, she won't make so many mistakes in the future.

Many of us are like Monica. We feel stuck with the hurts of our past. As we move into Step Eight, the first person we need to make amends to is ourself. We need to look at our pasts graciously and work to forgive ourselves.

Forgiving ourself will not start with some sweet, wonderful feeling. Forgiveness requires a decision that we make as an act of our will. It means that we give up the anger and resentment in our hearts and stop trying to punish ourselves for the past.

Before we seek forgiveness from others, we need to learn to forgive ourselves.

CSH

Then Peter came to Him and said, "Lord, how often
shall my brother sin against me, and I forgive him?
Up to seven times?" Jesus said . . . "I do not say to
you, up to seven times, but up to seventy times
seven."
                                    —MATT. 18:21–22

In the movie *A Man Called Peter,* the story of the great
Presbyterian preacher Peter Marshall, there is a scene
where his wife Catherine is ill. She writes letters to
everyone in her past, asking for their forgiveness for
some harm she felt she had done them.

This reminds me of Step Eight of the Twelve Steps.
Making a list of all persons we have harmed can be
pretty painful. Most of us would include our parents,
friends, brothers and sisters, and even people at work.
Some of us could have a list with only one name on it—
our own.

We may have harmed others physically in a moment
of anger. We may have harmed others verbally by saying something critical or sarcastic. We may have
harmed others emotionally just by not being there for
them when they needed us.

Now is the time to ask forgiveness. Those we
harmed need to know that we acknowledge our behavior.

———————————

There is forgiveness for every sin except the sin of not loving the Lord.
                                                    BLB

> *One often learns more from ten days of agony than
> from ten years of contentment.*
> —MERLE SHAIN

One afternoon while baking cookies Anita burned
her hand. She immediately placed her hand under cold
water, but the pain continued. She then held an ice-
pack on the damaged area. The ice seemed to numb
the pain, but each time Anita removed the pack the
burning would return. Anita finally realized that the
passage of time was the only thing that would completely stop her pain.

At the Twelve-Step meeting that night she shared
the valuable lesson she learned from her burn: Some of
the hurts that we can now acknowledge will only stop
hurting with time.

It hurts to realize how many people we harmed in
the past. We sought immediate relief without consider-
ing the impact of our behavior on others. In recovery
we learn to recognize, accept, and deal with our
feelings.

Our support groups and healthy behaviors are like
holding ice on a burn. They provide relief, but they are
not a "quick fix." We don't have to be discouraged
when pain takes time to heal.

---

*Pain makes us aware of our need for God to lead us and for people to
support us.*

CSH

Though I speak with the tongues of men and of
angels, but have not love, I have become as
sounding brass or a clanging symbol.
                                    —1 COR. 13:1

In Al-Anon you hear the phrase "Love the alcoholic;
hate the disease." This is important for your recovery.
Paul wrote to the Corinthians in 1 Corinthians 13, that
love has many dimensions:

> *Love is patient,*
> *Love is kind,*
> *Love does not envy,*
> *Love is not conceited,*
> *Love behaves in a seemly fashion,*
> *Love does not seek only for itself,*
> *Love is not provoked to anger,*
> *Love is not evil,*
> *Love rejoices with the truth.*

When someone we love is dying of cancer we are
kind and caring. Someone dying of alcoholism needs
love, kindness, and caring too. Love is hard to give
when you are at the end of your patience. That is why
we call on God for the strength to make amends to
those we have harmed. When you and your loved ones
are recovering, the love you feel is one of rejoicing.

The withholding of love is a negation of the Spirit of Christ in you, the
proof that you do not know him.

                                                        BLB

Submitting to one another in the fear of God.
                              —EPH. 5:21

Ann has a habit of not listening when her husband Cliff is speaking. She believes she has Cliff all figured out, so she starts to prepare her response before he even finishes talking. This habit has caused a lot of conflict in the marriage. Ann needs to learn that making amends with Cliff will require listening and not jumping to conclusions.

Common courtesy teaches us to listen and consider the opinions, thoughts, and plans of others. We feel free to learn from others when we consider that God is working in their lives too. If we treat others with respect, we often receive respect in return.

To stop controlling requires an active choice which frees other people to be themselves. When we let go, it provides a special testimony to others of the healing that God produces in our lives.

There is a real freedom in letting go of control of another person and letting them be themselves.

                                        CSH

> *"Judge not, and you shall not be judged. Condemn
> not, and you shall not be condemned. Forgive, and
> you will be forgiven."*   —LUKE 6:37

When we are preoccupied with another's problems
and we're trying to make them be like we think they
should be, we become obsessed with our job. This obsession takes over our personality and we are driven to
accomplish our goal. During this time we pay no attention to our own behavior. We neglect some of the characteristics in our own personality that are unhealthy,
such as nagging, whining, pouting, withdrawing, boss-
ing, raging, ignoring, criticizing, judging, manipulating, and withholding love.

Do any of these behaviors work? Of course not, so
why use them? Take one of them and try to change it
by practicing a healthy behavior in its place. Instead of
nagging, keep your mouth closed. When you speak,
speak in a loving and caring way. Instead of pouting,
put on a happy face. The Lord is much more concerned
with our critical ways than the behavior we judge of-
fensive in another.

---

*Many things must thou pass by with a deaf ear, and think rather of
the things that are for thy peace. It is more profitable to turn away
thine eyes from such things as displease thee than to be a slave to
contention (Thomas á Kempis).*

BLB

> *"Again I will build you, and you shall be rebuilt . . .*
> *And shall go forth in the dances of those who*
> *rejoice."*
>   —JER. 31:4

Until I allowed myself to feel and talk about the painful memories of my childhood, I was unable to know joy. Anyone can fake happiness. Now, through embracing the pain, I can now embrace real joy! In my life as a Christian, I needed to face my sin and realize the hurt and disappointment I caused God and others. Only then could I learn to face myself and feel love toward myself.

Taking a careful look at the past teaches us not to place blame on ourselves or produce guilt. Instead we learn to take responsibility for the hurt we caused ourselves and others. We honestly face the damage created by our dysfunctional lifestyle. Through feeling the pain of the past, we can finally remember it without it hurting us. We are then ready to make amends with the other people who were hurt by our behavior.

Lord, give me the courage to face all the areas of my life, especially the painful ones, so that you can restore me and rebuild my life.

                                                        CSH

Love . . . bears all things, believes all things, hopes all things, endures all things.

—1 COR. 13:4–7

When we focus our thoughts on God, our blessings become more than we can count. Is it possible to count every blessing in our life?

Sometimes when standing at the seashore we try to count the waves. Just as the waves and seashells wash to and fro, so do our blessings come and go. At good times in our life it is easy to count our blessings. We are thankful for health, family, friends, jobs, homes, church, community, and country.

God tells us we will have troubled times as well as good times. We compare the difficult times in our lives to the rough swells of the waves that rock and pound upon our feet. It becomes difficult to maintain our balance. As the waves wash against us they make us tumble and fall backward.

At times like this we have to maintain our balance with the weight of the memory of our blessings. Think of each blessing as an anchor. The anchor, a blessing, is dropped into the water. The anchor is heavy and unmovable, it stabilizes us against the waves.

Let us count our blessings one by one as they come to us from God (Myrna Thompson).

BLB

*"And just as you want men to do to you, you also
do to them likewise."*   —LUKE 6:31

Stacey sat with her face in her hands and wept. She
felt all jumbled up and confused. She knew that she
needed to make amends with her estranged sister,
Joyce, but Joyce wasn't even in recovery. Stacey
wanted to move forward in the steps, but she felt unwilling to admit her past failures to Joyce. She feared
that Joyce would laugh or make hurtful remarks at her
attempt to make amends.

Stacey prayed for willingness to seek forgiveness
from Joyce. She decided that she could not control
Joyce's response, but she was responsible for her own
recovery.

After talking with her group and seeking advice,
Stacey decided to write Joyce a letter asking forgiveness. That way Stacey could offer amends and yet set a
boundary that would protect her from Joyce's possible
unhealthy response.

---

*There are many ways to seek amends. God just asks for our will-
ingness.*

CSH

> *"A new commandment I give to you, that you love one another; as I have loved you, that you also love one another. By this all will know that you are My disciples, if you have love for one another."*
> —JOHN 13:34–35

It is easy to see how others have hurt us, but it's hard to see the harm in our actions to them likewise.

I do not often see our neighbor across the street. Once, when her husband died, I took a ham over for the family. Another time I saw her at a luncheon and spoke to her. Both times I was friendly; but what about the other days that I did not respond to her by calling or visiting? Was I being a friendly neighbor then?

Being a friendly neighbor entails showing others that you care about them by taking the time to tell them they are important to you.

In working Step Eight let us strive to be more consistent in our relationship with others.

BLB

The process of making revisions, particularly major revisions, is painful, sometimes excruciatingly painful.
                                        —SCOTT PECK

A dear friend of mine has a painful condition called "frozen shoulder." Left untreated, it can spread and immobilize both arms. The only cure is time, discipline, and patience with slow progress. Her treatments include heat, physical therapy, and daily stretching exercises. She has to push into the pain zone to reclaim her lost mobility.

Long ago, to avoid pain, some of us quit paying attention to our feelings and developed a condition called "frozen emotions." We have lost touch with our feelings.

In recovery we give ourselves permission to identify and reclaim our emotions, but it takes time and patience and the progress is slow. As we identify our feelings we become aware of our own hurts and the ways we have hurt others. We pursue health through the consistent daily exercise of practicing the Twelve Steps.

The exercise of recovery may be painful at times, but it produces healing.

                                                    CSH

*"Whenever you stand praying, if you have anything
against anyone, forgive him, that your Father in
heaven may also forgive you your trespasses."*
           —MARK 11:25

Anna came to the clinic for counseling because she
could see some of the behaviors that she didn't like
about herself being reflected in her children. She
would isolate herself by doing busywork, like needle-
point or sewing, in order not to face the emotional pain
of relationships. She even isolated from her family by
telling them she was too busy making something for
them to be bothered by them.

By isolating ourselves, we hurt not only others but
ourselves. We need to open up and let others come into
our life. If we are recovering from compulsive behavior, we need to let our light shine as we are healing so
that others can see the miracle of healing in our life. If
we are separated from God, now is the time to forgive
ourselves and stretch out to others and to God.

*Dear Lord, we ask you to come into our life, to mold us, and to make
us after your will.*

                                        BLB

> *Time wasted in getting even can never be used
> in getting ahead.* —ANONYMOUS

As Kelly turned forty she looked back over a past filled with broken relationships. Some of those relationships had left pain and had stayed in her thoughts for years. Kelly held onto deep resentments because she felt harmed and rejected. She tried to bury the pain of her broken heart in order to carry on with her life.

Step Eight required Kelly to take another look at these relationships. She had to dig up her broken heart and take responsibility for her part in the breakups. Although it was difficult to admit, she knew she played a part in the relationships breaking down.

Broken relationships find healing when we make amends. It may feel difficult, but we must accept responsibility when we have harmed someone. Honesty is necessary, even when the amends are not returned.

It always "takes two to tango." I am responsible for my part in relationships.

CSH

*Then Zacchaeus stood and said to the Lord, "Look,
Lord, I give half of my goods to the poor; and if I
have taken anything from anyone by false
accusation, I restore fourfold."*   —LUKE 19:8

When Eddie took his own inventory he came up with
the character defect of resentment. He wondered how
he could possibly make amends to all the people affected by his resentment. He resented Julie because he
thought she was better than he. He resented Mark because Mark didn't do things the way Eddie thought
they should be done. He resented Charlie because he
got along with Sarah better than Eddie did.

As he made his list for his inventory, he looked at
how he hurt himself by his resentment. By not being
open to people and their friendship, he lost out on having a warm relationship with someone. By not being
open to the different ways people work and solve problems, he lost out on learning new skills. By being afraid
of losing someone, he missed the chance of sharing a
friend with someone else.

———————————

*Lord, open our eyes to see those who have been sent to teach us your
way of love and caring.*

                                        BLB

If any of you lacks wisdom, let him ask of God,
who gives to all liberally and without reproach,
and it will be given to him.   —JAMES 1:5

One of the most common phrases heard from codependents is "I'm sorry." "I'm sorry that it's raining outside." "I'm sorry that I made you angry." "I'm sorry."

We frantically apologize for ourselves and for the behavior of other people. Eventually we feel overwhelmed with false guilt.

As we work Step Eight we need to avoid falling back into our extreme ways of thinking. The purpose of making a list of the people we have harmed is not to increase our feelings of guilt and shame. We need realistically to admit our wrong behavior while being gentle with ourselves.

God promised to give us wisdom if we ask for it. We need wisdom in this process to stay in balance and know the truth. It would be out of balance to list every person we ever met and apologize for who we are. The other extreme involves becoming defensive and placing total blame on others. The balance is to ask God for guidance as we honestly take responsibility for our own behavior.

_____

I no longer have to be sorry for who I am, but I do need to make amends with people I have harmed.

CSH

And be kind to one another, tenderhearted,
forgiving one another, just as God in Christ
also forgave you. —EPH. 4:32

Picture a boat that has been sitting in the water for a long time. The bottom of the boat is covered with barnacles, and the barnacles have gotten very hard. Their weight pulls the boat down into the water.

Our past mistakes are like barnacles. They cling to us and weigh us down. They prevent us from gliding through life with ease. To maintain the boat we have to knock the barnacles off and smooth out the hull. With confession to God we knock off our past mistakes, and by repentance we smooth out our lives.

As we are examining the things from the past that cling to us, we can identify the people we may have harmed by our attitude or behavior. Our intention here is to heal the past by confession and repentance. In this way we free ourselves from the mistakes and pain of relationships that may still be pulling us down. By letting go of the past, we can let God transform us in the present.

———————————

God has smoothed out our life by sending his Son to die for our mistakes.

BLB

"The price of wisdom is above rubies."
—JOB 28:18

Whenever our dog Jordan hears a cat, squirrel, or rustling leaf in the backyard, she takes off running in the direction of the noise. It does not matter to Jordan that her collar is attached to a chain. She runs at full speed, straight for her goal. Suddenly the chain pulls taut, and she is jerked to a painful halt. Jordan has never learned her limits.

God graciously gave each of us a conscience. Our conscience tugs on our heart whenever we go beyond healthy moral limits. Unlike Jordan's chain, it will not keep us from going too far.

God gives us guidelines in the Bible to teach us how to treat other people. He provides us with wisdom and conscience to see whom we may have hurt in the past. Learning from our past mistakes keeps us from repeating them in the future.

God gives us wisdom so that our conscience can help us realize the healthy boundaries he has set.

CSH

This being so, I myself always strive to have a conscience without offense toward God and men.
　　　　　　　　　　　　　　　　—ACTS 24:16

The apostle Paul's desire was to let his conscience guide his actions. All of us have consciences, too, and they can be powerful motivators that keep churning inside us until we're forced into some kind of action. Usually this action involves making a right out of a wrong.

When my daughter was young, she would complain about having Pac Man chomping away in her tummy every time she felt guilty about something. Of course, Pac Man went away as soon as she admitted her wrongdoing and made amends.

There are a lot of people we hurt as the years go by. Think for a moment about the various people you might have hurt in the past year. Usually family members will top the list. What about business associates, friends, and casual acquaintances? Grab the nearest piece of paper and jot down your victims' names as you think of them. Now, circle the names of a few people to whom you can begin making amends this week. Pray for guidance in each contact, and the Lord will surely bless your efforts.

Hurting and healing seems to be a familiar back-and-forth pattern for all of us. Focus on the healing side in the coming months.

FLM

> *Joy to forgive and joy to be forgiven hang level in*
> *the balance of love.* —RICHARD GARNETT

Forgiving others is not a natural human ability. We need humbly to come before God and explain to him the deep hurts of our hearts. We may need to start by praying for a willingness to forgive. We may actively pray about the same situation for a long time before we know that we have forgiven the wrongs of the past.

Once we have forgiven ourselves and others, we can start the process of asking others to forgive us for the hurts we caused. We take responsibility for the damage our actions produced in the lives of people in our past.

God is the author of forgiveness. He has graciously forgiven our sins through the death and resurrection of his Son, Jesus Christ. God wants us to show that same grace toward others by working through the process of forgiveness and then asking them to forgive us.

When we remember that God has forgiven us, we are motivated to ask others for forgiveness.

CSH

We made direct amends to such people wherever possible, except when to do so would injure them or others.

Martha and John have been married twenty years and have two teenagers. Martha is passive-aggressive, and John is dominant. The children, as teenagers will, seem to get into a lot of trouble. John handles discipline by verbally abusing the children or by hitting them with a belt. When the abuse is taking place, Martha goes to her room and cries, expresses her anger at John sarcastically, or acts passive and uncaring.

Through their Twelve-Step program, these parents learned to make amends and asked their children's forgiveness.

With God's help we can accept the past, forgive ourselves and others, and make changes in our own behavior. By turning our past behavior into positive nurturance of others, we can reap good things that come from a loving heart.

The time will come to reap the harvest. What seeds are you sowing?

BLB

The real fault is to have faults and not amend them.
                              —CONFUCIUS

During graduate school Frank and Lee were room-mates. Whenever Lee offered a suggestion about cleaning the apartment, Frank flew off the handle and yelled. Lee quickly learned not to mention problems to Frank, and after a year of living in a tense situation, Lee decided to move out.

Years later as Frank worked through recovery, he remembered the relationship with Lee. Because he now could feel his emotions, he realized how Lee must have felt attacked by his anger. Frank realized Lee only tried to help him, but Frank took Lee's ideas as personal criticism.

Frank called his university and found out how to contact Lee. Lee was surprised to hear from his old roommate, but he listened willingly as Frank explained his recovery process and asked for forgiveness. As Frank hung up the phone that day, he felt relieved of a burden from the past.

Our hearts feel lighter as we mend past relationships.

CSH

> *"Blessed are the peacemakers,*
> *For they shall be called sons of God."*
> —MATT. 5:9

During active alcoholism in a family, damage is done to relationships between parent and child and between husband and wife. After recovery these relationships need to be healed, and we also need to develop tools for making new relationships. This can be a rewarding part of our recovery.

Alan Loy McGinnis in the book *The Friendship Factor* offers some ideas that help make the process a little easier. He writes about tools to use during communication. He says you can listen with your eyes and make body contact with people by touching their hands or arms. While talking with them, it helps to tell them how much you appreciate them or how well they did something. Sometimes we interrupt people because we want to talk with them and they may have their mind on something else. McGinnis suggests that we schedule time to talk with people so that they can be ready to talk to us. Listening is a major part of any conversation. McGinnis suggests that we listen with affection and don't try to argue or change the subject.

―――――――――

Make someone's day healthier. Affirmations are a great prescription for one's self-image.

BLB

We love Him because He first loved us.
—1 JOHN 4:19

Most people have had a lot of questions about friendships. How do we really know a friend? We can't seem to find a single relationship in which we don't feel, at some time, like the person disappoints us. We also realize that we have let many of our friends down. We question God at that point, and we ask him his purpose in friendships.

God's purpose in friendship is not to satisfy our need for love. We find freedom through learning that we cannot satisfy anyone else's need for love, and they cannot satisfy our need. God wants to satisfy that need! But the people in our lives are our greatest opportunity to show his love to others and to experience his love (through human form) for us.

The next time we feel unloved, instead of picking up the phone we could look at some "love letters" that God wrote to us in his Word. Then we feel ready to risk loving others because we know, in spite of their response to us, that we are loved by God.

Friends are God's way of taking really good care of us.

CSH

And though I have the gift of prophecy, and
understand all mysteries and all knowledge, and
though I have all faith, so that I could remove
mountains, but have not love, I am nothing.
—1 COR. 13:2

God tells us that no matter how talented or smart we are, without love we are nothing.

Because of a misunderstanding Jane and Laura lost their friendship. Jane's son had done some remodeling work for Laura, and there was a misunderstanding about when the work was to be completed. Laura and her husband got very angry and fired the young man. Jane and her husband tried to help solve the problem, but there was too much anger on both sides.

Because of anger or hurt feelings we sometimes lose ones we love. Because we hang on to hurt feelings, they can become so engrained in our personality that we become bitter. This bitterness can become like poison that kills our soul. We need to look at the events that have caused the anger and be willing to seek the truth. Our healing will come from forgiving harm done to us and by making amends for harm we have done to others.

God wants us to have a willing heart, and he will fill it up with love.
BLB

Weeping may endure for a night,
But joy comes in the morning.
—PS. 30:5

Our feelings are important. Many of us remember the expression, "Sticks and stones may break my bones, but words will never hurt me." We were instructed to use this as a reply whenever someone would say something that hurt our feelings. The truth is, words *can* hurt! The word or touch of an unkind person cannot damage our life if we learn how to tell someone safe about the feelings on the inside.

Talking to some three-year-olds about safe touches, a counselor asked the question, "How do we get our feelings from the inside to the outside?" A little girl raised her hand. "Through our eyes," she answered while using her hands to show the tears that come down her cheeks. A little boy said, "Through our mouth." Ah yes, with words—telling someone how we feel and letting them share our tears.

Let us learn from the example of these children to express our feelings, even when the emotions are painful.

CSH

Now may the God of patience and comfort grant
you to be like-minded toward one another,
according to Christ Jesus.   —ROM. 15:5

During times of emotional stress Joan would neglect others as she focused on her own feelings of loneliness, fear, and rejection. Her husband was an alcoholic, and she reacted to his behavior by withdrawing emotionally from him and her children. When she heard in Al-Anon that she needed to make amends to those she hurt, she first responded, "Well, what about someone apologizing to me?" The anger at what caused her pain was the first emotion to be expressed. Deep down it really hurt when she had to stop and look at what her behavior had done to her spouse and her children.

How do we mend these hurts? Step Nine tells us to make amends to those we have hurt, unless to do so would hurt them further. Joan told her children and spouse how sorry she was to have shut them out of her life. Tremendous healing took place in that family once they all were able to communicate with each other.

Communication opens the door to forgiveness. Forgiveness leads to healing.

BLB

Those who sow in tears
Shall reap in joy.
—PS. 126:5

We take responsibility for our own behavior by making amends. We need a clear understanding of the reason for our apology. It takes time to decide the healthiest way to say we are sorry.

After we completed Step Eight, God provides us with wisdom to move forward into Step Nine. The goal of this step is to free us from guilt and bring us to a place of peace and forgiveness.

At certain times we need to apologize specifically for the wrong behaviors of our past. At other times we need to recognize our responsibility in part of a problem that brought pain to others.

Ephesians 4:15 tells us to speak the truth in love. There is no need to be critical or blaming of our past behavior. That only adds to our poor self-esteem. We can accept responsibility for our wrongs without condemning ourselves. Our sorrow over the past leads us to future joy.

_____

Because God has forgiven us, we are free to forgive ourselves and others.

CSH

Behold, how good and how pleasant it is
For brethren to dwell together in unity!
—PS. 133:1

Over the years God has sent people to give me special gifts. One grandmother taught me the love of reading. The other one took me with her to her Sunday school class. Later, other people came into my life to teach me special things. The music teacher I had in junior high taught me to love music. The couple who served as youth ministers at our church and the ladies I served with at the Girl Scout day camp all taught me to laugh and have fun outdoors. The summer I studied under Carl Rogers, I learned to listen. The special friends I worked with at Southern Methodist University taught me how to support and encourage others in a work setting.

I have grown to appreciate these gifts as heavenly treasures. Making amends also means telling those who have helped you how much you appreciate their friendship and help.

Thank your special friends for the gifts that are assurances of God's love.

BLB

Forgiveness is a gift I give myself.
—ANONYMOUS

Forgiveness is hard to understand and difficult to carry out. Some of us were taught to "forgive and forget," and we feel guilty when we realize that concept is not possible. Others of us were taught never to forgive and to make certain we got revenge on people who had wronged us.

When we are unwilling to forgive, resentment grows in our hearts. Resentment damages the person who keeps it. It steals away our joy for life and robs us of the energy we need to celebrate each moment. Often the people we refuse to forgive aren't even aware of our resentment. We become victims of ourselves when we choose not to forgive others.

The act of forgiveness is not based on a feeling. Forgiveness is an act of our will. Deciding to forgive produces healthy feelings later on. By forgiving others, we decide not to be damaged any longer by the wrongdoings of the past. The people who wronged us may not deserve to be forgiven, but we don't deserve God's forgiveness either.

_____

Learning to forgive others allows us to show grace toward others in the same loving way God has shown grace to us by forgiving our sins.

CSH

> *Above all things have fervent love for one another,*
> *for "love will cover a multitude of sins."*
>   —1 PETER 4:8

Yvonne was addicted to perfectionism. This perfectionism was exhibited by her getting too involved in projects around the house, rather than having the time to just sit and listen and be with other family members. At work she was unable to accept the work her employees turned in. She always had to criticize the job or finish it the way she wanted it herself. She pushed people away from her with her anger and raged at their not doing things the way she thought they should be done.

In recovery she had to deal with her behavior. She began by making amends to her family and to her subordinates at work. Then she needed to change her behavior toward them. The reward was that, in making these changes, she learned to love herself better because she was free of guilt.

_____

Try not to become a person of success but rather a person of value (Albert Einstein).

                                                        BLB

In dealing with other people remember the three C's: you didn't cause it, you can't control it, and you can't cure it.   —LORNA P.

During my college years I worked as a lifeguard and learned about rescuing people. If a person became distressed in water where he could not stand safely on the bottom, he was in danger of drowning. It was then necessary for me to dive in and pull him to safety.

On the other hand, if an adult started to thrash around and panic in shallow water, he usually did not need to be rescued. Instead, he needed to hear me yell for him to put his feet down on the bottom. His panic left the minute his foot touched the concrete, and he realized that he had safely taken care of himself.

For years many of us have rescued people who are not really helpless. We build our own feelings of worth thinking we are being helpful. But the truth is we are really doing damage when we needlessly rescue others. We damage ourselves because we use up a lot of needed energy and forget to take care of ourselves.

We do an injustice to those we rescue, because they become dependent and never learn that they can take care of themselves.

CSH

> *The wise in heart will be called prudent,*
> *And sweetness of the lips increases learning.*
> *Understanding is a wellspring of life to him*
>   *who has it.*
> *But the correction of fools is folly.*
> *The heart of the wise teaches his mouth,*
> *And adds learning to his lips.*
> *Pleasant words are like a honeycomb,*
> *Sweetness to the soul and health to the bones.*
>   —PROV. 16:21–24

As we grow in recovery we become wiser in the ways of the Lord. A good way to learn healthy ways to live our lives is by reading the Proverbs of Solomon, the son of King David. There is one for each day of the month so you can pick up your Bible any day of the month and read the Proverb chapter that is the same as the date.

In Step Nine, as in Proverbs, we learn the wisdom to make appropriate amends. We want to make amends wherever possible, except when to do so would injure them or others. Also in the Twelve-Step program, as in Proverbs, we learn how to live one day at a time. We cannot change the past, and tomorrow has not yet come. Proverbs and the Twelve-Step program give us tools to use in our own relationships with our family, friends, and co-workers.

Wisdom can never be taken away from us.

BLB

He shall cover you with His feathers,
And under His wings you shall take refuge.
—PS. 91:4a

During a storm or when faced with a predator, a mother hen instinctively spreads her wings so that her baby chicks can run underneath to safety. She covers them with her feathers in order to save their lives. The hen will risk her own life in order to provide a place of safety and shelter for her chicks.

Each of us longs to feel protected and safe while we seek to make amends. Psalm 91:4 describes how God desires to provide a refuge for us. A refuge is a place of shelter and protection during a time of danger or difficulty. Just as the mother hen protects her young, so God stands ready to love us and protect us. We can draw strength from God when we feel nervous, uncertain, or afraid while making apologies to those we hurt in the past.

God is a trustworthy shelter in times of difficulty. We can turn to him to provide safety.

CSH

Do not withhold good from those to whom it is due,
When it is in the power of your hand to do so.
         —PROV. 3:27

Making amends to others is a little more involved than just a simple "I'm sorry." John wanted to make amends, but the person he wanted to apologize to was no longer in his life. Making amends was impossible because the person had died, but through prayer and writing he communicated his feelings over the wrong done to this person. After committing his thoughts to paper he did something kind for someone else.

Margaret needed to make amends to her immediate family. She didn't know how they were going to accept what she had to say, but she wanted to try to repair the damage done to them by her words and her actions. Before attempting this process, she needed to call upon the healing power of the Lord to guide her in what she said.

As we list those we have harmed and begin making amends to them, we should remember that we need time and patience in which to grow ourselves. In some circumstances we should not rush in and abruptly try to mend a broken fence.

———————

With God's help grow in love, understanding, and patience and change what you can.

          BLB

Let us not grow weary while doing good, for in due season we shall reap.   —GAL. 6:9

Farmers have a tremendous amount of patience. Their job requires working for a long time without seeing any results. They have faith that plowing up the soil, planting the seeds, watering the fields, and fertilizing the crop will eventually produce a harvest as the fruit of their labor.

God encourages us to not grow weary while doing good. We easily feel overwhelmed or discouraged as we seek to make amends. Some people may still feel bitter about our past mistakes and refuse to accept our apology.

The verse today reminds us that eventually we will reap a harvest. Sometimes the fruit will be a restored relationship, and sometimes it will be the peace of knowing we asked for forgiveness.

We seek to make amends but leave the results to God.

CSH

*Now concerning things offered to idols: We know
that we all have knowledge. Knowledge puffs up,
but love edifies. And if anyone thinks that he knows
anything, he knows nothing yet as he ought to
know. But if anyone loves God, this one is known
by Him.*   —1 COR. 8:1–3

Alice was told, "Every time you open your mouth,
your mind goes on parade for all to see." She was a
know-it-all who charged through life without any re-
gard to her impact on others. She had a lot of knowledge in certain areas, but it was not until she had the
knowledge of Christ that she was able to turn her life
around. With this, she learned to relate to people
through love and caring.

Love doesn't blow up—it fills up. It's a nurturing food
that builds and lasts. Love for God led Alice to love for
others. Love began to determine her relationships with
others.

Start improving your relationships by letting God
help you with your attitudes toward your peers, your
authorities, your dependents, and yourself.

*Our lives should be governed by love—love of God, love of others, and
love of self.*

                                                      FLM

When there is a fire, the rules change.
—DR. LANE OGDEN

The owner of my office building would get very upset if I decided to throw a chair through my window. Yet if the building was on fire, I would receive applause for breaking out windows in order to save myself.

Many of us grew up with an internal pain that felt like an emotional fire. Some of the behaviors we used to save ourselves, like dependency in relationships or the abuse of mood-altering substances, caused damage to other people.

Now that we have found healing for our hearts, we need to make amends with the people we hurt during the "fire." We humbly ask their forgiveness for causing pain in their lives. After damage occurs, there is a need for rebuilding.

_____

Pursue peace with all men (Heb. 12:14).

CSH

*Therefore, as the elect of God, holy and beloved,
put on tender mercies, kindness, humbleness of
mind, meekness, longsuffering; bearing with one
another, and forgiving one another, if anyone has a
complaint against another; even as Christ forgave
you, so you also must do.*   —COL. 3:12–13

John was truly sorry for the way he had hurt Mary
while he was drinking. He sat down across the kitchen
table, looked Mary in the eye, and said, "Mary, I want
you to know that I am truly sorry for the way I hurt you
when I was drinking. Someday, I hope you can find it in
your heart to forgive me." Then he proceeded to treat
her with respect and love whenever they were together. One day Mary healed from her pain, and she
was able not only to forgive, but to feel love for John
again. The amends, followed by a change in behavior,
was the key.

John had first spent time in prayer. He had reflected
on his own feelings and asked for wisdom to choose
the right words and the power to accept the consequences. Using the power of the program, he made
amends in an honest and caring way.

*Begin with prayer, communicate with love, and end with forgiveness
toward yourself and others.*

BLB

Let each become all that he is capable of being . . .
expand, if possible, to his full growth.
                              —THOMAS CARLYLE

When the Stolz family purchased a thirty-year-old home, they were delighted by the potential beauty it held. Their joy turned to frustration one afternoon as they worked outside. The flower beds had received no attention for years. The gardens were filled with weeds and lots of soggy dead leaves. They had to accept that it would take a lot of time and hard work before the gardens could have beauty again.

Entering Step Nine clears out years of old habits in our lives. Just like the unkept garden, we must clean out and discard the dead leaves of our past. As we admit our faults and acknowledge the damage of our wrongs, then we can ask for forgiveness from those people we damaged.

As amends are made and the garbage of the past is cleared out of our lives, we will find fertile ground in which to plant a new lifestyle of serenity.

                                                    CSH

> *"You have heard that it was said, 'You shall love*
> *your neighbor and hate your enemy.' But I say to*
> *you, love your enemies, bless those who curse you,*
> *do good to those who hate you, and pray for those*
> *who spitefully use you and persecute you."*
>
> —MATT. 5:43–44

Laura grew up with an alcoholic father who verbally abused her. He criticized her behavior, her looks, and other things about her. As Laura grew older, she learned to hide her feelings and stay away from his critical eye. She went away to college and never returned to her home town. Laura's father grieved the loss of his daughter but did not have the power to get her to come see him.

One day a miracle happened. He quit drinking and became involved in the Twelve-Step program of Alcoholics Anonymous. As he became willing to turn his life and his will over to the power of God, he began to change. He called his daughter to make amends for all the hurt he had caused her. At first she wouldn't return his calls. The wall she had built to protect herself from him was pretty thick. He kept reaching out to her with love, and eventually with the power of God, he was able to talk with her and enter her life again.

Only the power of God can turn a wall into a door and push it open.

BLB

*Let us lay aside every weight, and the sin which so
easily ensnares us, and let us run with endurance
the race that is set before us.*   —HEB. 12:1

When Olympic runners compete, they wear the lightest clothing possible. Athletes would never consider running in a full suit of armor or while carrying along a thirty-pound suitcase. Such extra weight would cause them to finish last or even to drop out of the race.

The verse today tells us to get rid of anything that weighs us down and keeps us from running. Making amends and asking forgiveness from people we have harmed gets rid of the burdens that are so heavy and allows us to move forward toward our goals.

Once we are freed from excess baggage, we can focus our attention on becoming more like Christ every day.

                                                    CSH

Let nothing be done through selfish ambition or conceit, but in lowliness of mind let each esteem others better than himself. Let each of you look out not only for his own interests, but also for the interests of others.   —PHIL. 2:3–4

Have you ever heard the statement, "It's easy for you to say I'm sorry; you say it all the time"? Sometimes we do repeat the same unhealthy behavior over and over, say we're sorry when confronted, and then keep on behaving in the same way. Making amends can mean just changing an inappropriate behavior that we keep repeating.

For example, Sharon is consistently late. Subconsciously Sharon is saying that her time is of more value than the other person's time. Others cannot trust her to do what she says she will do. Instead of repeatedly apologizing, Sharon should change her behavior and work on being on time for appointments, meetings, or social engagements.

In order to change our behavior, we need to practice a new behavior every day for twenty-one days and let it become a habit. Habits can be learned and can also be unlearned. Remember that you are in control of your choices and you can change.

With God's help, we can do anything one minute at a time or one day at a time.

BLB

The task ahead of us is never as great as the Power behind us.
                                        —ANONYMOUS

Several years ago my parents gave me a regulator clock. In the past year the clock has caused me great frustration. Winding it once supposedly keeps it working for eight days. However, often I wind the clock only to find that it soon stops running. The momentum of the pendulum produces the energy for the clock to run, but something is causing the pendulum to stop swinging.

We can be similar to the clock in our recovery process. As we enter the program, we are driven by the energy of wanting to change and work through our addictions. As time goes on and we move further into the steps, we often grow weary with the amount of fear and pain we have to face. Discouragement can lead us to feel overwhelmed at times, and this begins to slow down our momentum.

Just as the clock needs to be repaired by someone who understands clocks, so we too need encouragement and motivation from people who understand the program.

We can look to those people who are farther along in their recovery to help us regain the energy and momentum to continue moving forward in our recovery process.

                                                        CSH

Who are you to judge another's servant? To his
own master he stands or falls. Indeed, he will be
made to stand, for God is able to make him stand.
                                        —ROM. 14:4

Rosemary is a single mother with a son who is now
twenty-one years old. He has a problem with alcohol
and drugs. He has dropped out of college, is on proba-
tion for driving while drinking, and has been involved
in numerous wrecks. These problems did not happen
overnight. They began years ago.

Rosemary grew up with a fear of abandonment. Her
father was in the Navy and was gone a lot when she
was a child. As she went through relationships herself,
she attempted to control the people she was involved
with so that they could not abandon her.

By making amends with her son and letting him go
to choose help for himself, Rosemary broke the chain
of dependency.

Where do we begin to stop unhealthy behavior that
affects generation after generation? The only place to
begin is with ourselves.

We cannot change another person; we can only change ourselves.
Only through our conscious contact with God can we gain the wis-
dom to know where to begin.

                                                    BLB

*The healthier we become, the less willing we
become to tolerate disaster in our relationships.*
—MARY CATHERINE NORTH

Tony made Maria the center of his world. All of his
energy was focused on pleasing Maria and gaining her
approval. Whenever she was happy, Tony felt happy.
When Maria was depressed, he felt depressed.

Dependent relationships are similar to putting all
your eggs in one basket. If you give one person your
emotional basket, it will be a disaster when he drops
the basket, because every egg will break.

Our emotional health grows as we learn to divide
our needs into several relationships. When we have
several intimate friendships, we gain a better perspective by listening to different opinions.

Throughout life people will leave us due to reloca-
tion, death, and possibly through misunderstandings.
If we place all our dependency on one person, we will
feel devastated. On the other hand, if we balance our
friendships, we will experience a loss, but we will still
have a healthy support system.

Relationships are only as healthy as the people in them.

CSH

*So then, each of us shall give account of himself
to God. Therefore let us not judge one another
anymore, but rather resolve this, not to put
a stumbling block or a cause to fall in our
brother's way.*
—ROM. 14:12–13

After you have been in the Twelve-Step program for some time, you may begin to have uneasy feelings when you are with the people you knew before you became sober. You need to make amends to them for your previous behavior. Do not be judgmental or critical of them and their part in the relationship.

It is also very important to go to your meetings as often as possible. In Alcoholics Anonymous they say "ninety meetings in ninety days" at the beginning. This frequency gives you support and encouragement as you learn a new way of relating to those you care about. As you try to return to your former circle of friends, you may be tempted to return to your old habits with them. If this happens, forgive yourself and get back into the program quickly.

The answer for us is in doing God's will, not our will.

BLB

"They have forsaken Me, the fountain of living waters."
—JER. 2:13

During recovery, we come to understand our thirst to be listened to. For years we kept secrets, and now we learn that healing occurs only through sharing our past and making amends.

Imagine yourself in the desert without water, overcome with thirst. Suddenly a waterfall appears! Clean, clear water, as much as you need or want! You become satisfied, full, drenched. Surely you cannot stay in the waterfall forever. But what if you become thirsty again back in the desert? What guarantee do you have that your thirst will be met? As you move through different stages of recovery, you may wonder if God will provide a person when you develop a new thirst to be heard.

In the Bible, a woman went to draw water from a well because she was thirsty. Jesus told her, "Whoever drinks of the water that I shall give him will never thirst" (John 4:14). God knows all our needs and understands us intimately. His offer of living water is still available to each of us today.

_____

God, help me to accept the Water of Life that you want to give me, so that I can enjoy relationships with others and not use them to quench my thirst.

CSH

See that no one renders evil for evil to anyone, but always pursue what is good both for yourselves and for all.   —1 THESS. 5:15

As John and Mary worked through the Twelve-Step program, they began to see little changes take place—changes in their relationship with each other, new feelings about themselves, and insights into their own attitudes and behavior. John was able to heal through forgiveness of himself and others. Mary learned to accept herself and to quit trying to change people.

As Mary looked at her strengths and weaknesses and worked to change her weaknesses, she began to like herself better. John stopped looking at the wrong done to him and started looking at the harm he had done to others by his actions and words. They both began to develop a sense of value about themselves. Then they began to expect others to value them also.

As you turn your life around, this time choose happiness and love yourself.

BLB

> *Blessed are the peacemakers,*
> *For they shall be called sons of God.*
> —MATT. 5:9

Nancy found out that disappointment comes when there is a big space between fantasy and reality. She had often orchestrated her life as if it were a fairy tale. She wrote the script, cast the characters, and tried to direct the scene.

Since Nancy had grown up in a pain-filled family, the scene in her fantasy was a dinner table surrounded by laughing, happy people sharing experiences. The reality was a scene with all members of the family focused on the out-of-control behavior of one member. She felt a sense of powerlessness when she tried to create her fantasy. Soon she became aware that it was like the powerlessness she felt when she tried to control others.

We should love and forgive the characters who play the family roles, and we should also forgive ourselves for trying to control others. We need to see the reality in our relationships and not build our relationships on fantasy.

Acceptance frees us to change. Change frees us to see reality.

BLB

*We continued to take personal inventory, and when
we were wrong, promptly admitted it.*

When Betty came in for counseling, she was angry at
her husband for all the things he didn't do to make her
happy. I would try to get her to talk about her reactions
to her husband, but all she could do was list his faults.

When she related an incident when she had become
upset at her husband, I asked her why she reacted that
way. She said, "He didn't do what I wanted him to do." I
asked her to look at her expectations rather than his
behavior. She saw that she was trying to control him
because she felt so out of control herself.

As she continued in therapy, she became more
aware of her need to change and with the help of the
Lord, day by day, she was able to become the loving,
supportive wife she really wanted to be.

---

*Sometimes we need to turn around and look at the situation from a
different perspective.*

FLM

*Forgetting those things which are behind and
reaching forward to those things which are ahead.*
—PHIL. 3:13

My mother used to collect Green Stamps. She received a certain number of points in stamps from the grocery store based on the amount of her purchase. These valuable tokens were pasted into stamp books. Items were purchased from the Green Stamp catalog by redeeming her completed books of stamps.

Many of us are like Green Stamp collectors when it comes to our anger. We keep a mental record of each time we feel wronged. Just as the stamps had a value of 5, 10, or 50 points, we assign point levels to the anger we store toward other people.

We have a right to be angry about abuses in our past, but we also need to deal with the issues so that we can stop dragging them around. Bringing up the past is not a fair style of fighting. People in intimate relationships will all have disagreements at one time or another, but we need to learn to discuss current problems without bringing up those from the past.

I will work to let go of my anger and release it to God. My goal is to enjoy today instead of living in the past.

CSH

*For it is God who works in you both to will and to
do for His good pleasure.*   —PHIL. 2:13

Jack did not want to drink, but he was addicted to
alcohol. He craved it and could not give it up. He
searched for a power greater than the willpower he
had to help him give up drinking. Then he met Philip, a
minister who has worked with recovering alcoholics
for many years. Philip told Jack that the strength for
success was not his. It could only be found by serving
the Lord.

Today, Jack is successful in his recovery. He has not
had a drink in seven years, and through his church and
his devotional time he has been able to use the power
of the Lord to keep him sober. He serves his church,
helps others who are struggling, and has learned to
take care of himself. He is dedicated to serving the
Lord; God works in him and through him according to
God's will.

————————

*Success cannot be achieved by our will, but by the might and power
of God working in us.*

FLM

No temptation has overtaken you except such as is common to man; but God is faithful, who will not allow you to be tempted beyond what you are able, but with the temptation will also make the way of escape, that you may be able to bear it.
—1 COR. 10:13

Sometimes we feel like we are alone in our pain. We draw in and isolate ourselves, thinking that in so doing we will heal alone. But think of the healing process of a badly infected cut on your arm or leg. The cut has been a painful invasion of your physical body. The doctor treats the infection and, after a while, uncovers the wound and exposes it to the air. Then it seems that the pain and infection go away quickly.

This is the same treatment for the emotional pain of broken relationships. The cut has been a deep invasion of your emotional being. This cut can be treated by a professional counselor, a minister, or a caring friend. After sharing the pain, you are emotionally ready for exposure to a new relationship. This exposure will quickly aid the healing process.

We can cure our pain by risking the experience of reaching out to others.

BLB

I love the LORD because He has heard
My voice and my supplications.
Because He has inclined His ear to me,
Therefore I will call upon Him as long as I live.
—PS. 116:1–2

God answers prayer—not always the way we want him to, but he does answer. Writing letters to God is a very good way to keep a record of your prayers. In your letter you can pour out your heart and then set the letter aside and wait for God's answer. On rainy days when I'm home and feeling a little lonely, I open my journal of "Dear God" letters, read through them, and rejoice in the glory of his answers. As I read each letter, I write the answer at the bottom of the page to remind me of his answers. I call these answers "mini miracles," because he heard and he answered.

As we communicate daily with God about our personal life, we need to admit when we are wrong and ask for forgiveness. But communication with God has to work both ways. We call that meditation time. There needs to be time for confession but there also needs to be time to accept forgiveness.

Dear God, I always ask you for something. Today I will strive to hear what you have to say.

BLB

Out of the same mouth proceed blessing and
cursing. My brethren, these things ought not
to be so.   —JAMES 3:10

While watching news reports on the Persian Gulf crisis, I was amazed at the size of the aircraft carriers and destroyers in the naval fleet. It is astounding to realize that the captains of these huge ships direct the ships' movement by controlling a small rudder.

The book of James compares the rudder of a ship to our tongue. Even though our tongue is small in comparison to our entire body, it can be the most powerful part of our body. Once words have come out of our mouth, they can never be taken back. Our words can do severe damage to other people.

As we work in recovery, the anger and hurt start to leave our hearts so that they no longer fuel our words. We become aware of any harmful patterns we developed in our speech. God desires to give us wisdom in taming our tongue so that we can speak the truth in a loving way and learn to verbally encourage ourselves and others.

_____

I will seek to be aware of the power of the tongue so that I can speak
a blessing to myself and others.

                                                              CSH

When I was a child, I spoke as a child, I understood as a child, I thought as a child; but when I became a man, I put away childish things. For now we see in a mirror, dimly, but then face to face. Now I know in part, but then I shall know just as I also am known.   —1 COR. 13:11–12

When I was a child I spoke, thought, and acted in childish ways; but now that I am grown, I wonder sometimes if I have put away all of those childish things. Don't I still enjoy surprises and feel excitement when a bird sings, trees sway, and the wind softly blows on my face? Do we become wiser as we grow older? We certainly learn more with each passing year, but let's hope we still retain the childish excitement we feel when we see nature, hear children's laughter, and feel the warmth of sunshine on our face. Being open to the childlike spirit and love of life allows us to be open to change in our own thoughts and actions. Knowing that God is always with us gives us hope that we can change. It is up to us to make each age of our life an important time.

We ask that with God's help we may live our lives one day at a time (Myrna Thompson).

BLB

> *In the process of growing to spiritual maturity, we
> all go through many adolescent stages.*
> —MIKI L. BOWEN

For some of us the very term *adolescence* sounds like chaos. Teens are trapped in change they don't understand. We can support them by giving them permission to experience the trauma of growing up. Given love and time, they will emerge as whole persons equipped for healthy adult life.

Many of us who were raised in dysfunctional homes never received that kind of support. We became what our elders wanted or we inappropriately rebelled. Either way, we learned to hide behind whatever coping skills helped us survive. Hence, we did not pass normally through the adolescent sorting years.

In recovery we give ourselves permission to go through a late adolescence. We need to sort and resort the data of our pasts. For a time, we may feel confused as the dysfunctional absolutes of the past give way to the flexible options of the future. These changes feel uncomfortable, but they are quite normal.

Today I can leave behind my unhealthy loyalty to the past and claim the me I was intended to be.

CSH

Whoever loves instruction loves knowledge,
But he who hates reproof is stupid.
                              —PROV. 12:1

Several years ago a man was applying for a job. The man who was interviewing him said, "You have told us about your strengths. Now let's talk about your weaknesses." The man sat back, thought for a few moments, and then replied, "I don't think I have any weaknesses." The interviewer said, "Oh, everyone has some weakness." The applicant replied again, "I don't think I have any weaknesses." The interviewer retorted, "Well, you must not be married, or you would know what they are."

We are often guilty of not looking into our own thoughts and behavior. In our program we make a fearless moral inventory of our characteristics; then we ask God to remove them. In Step Ten we continue to take daily inventories, and when we are wrong, we promptly admit it.

Our shortcomings are a part of who we are. Our main purpose in recovery is to change some of these thoughts and behaviors. We need daily to ask God for insight into our own thoughts and behavior.

We need to consciously set aside old habits and go shopping for healthier ones.

                                                    BLB

Ninety percent of life is just showing up.
—WOODY ALLEN

Soon after Tara and Kent started to date, they decided to learn to play tennis. As they hit the ball back and forth, Kent became angry with his lack of ability. Each time he swung and missed the ball his frustration increased. Finally he threw his racket to the ground and yelled, "I'm tired of doing this the wrong way!"

It wasn't right or wrong for Kent to miss the ball. It was simply evidence that he was just learning to play.

We are constantly learning healthy behaviors. Sometimes we will forget to nurture ourselves or practice the steps or set healthy boundaries. But forgetting won't be wrong. We can move forward and continue learning about recovery.

Accepting the process gives me courage to continue my progress.

CSH

*Be of the same mind toward one another. Do not
set your mind on high things, but associate with
the humble.*
                                    —ROM. 12:16

Today we hear the word *dysfunctional* tossed around. Webster's Dictionary defines *dys* as abnormal. *Functional* relates to acting. So *dysfunctional* means abnormal acting.

Janie comes from a dysfunctional family. Her father is alcoholic, and her mother is very quiet and distant. Her mother lives in constant fear of her father's drunken rages, and Janie has to take care of both her father and her mother. They all react to his behavior. This in itself is abnormal, because the focus is on an ill person and this person is setting the behavioral reactions of all the members of the family.

Janie has been affected by her family in that she has not received the love, nurturing, and encouragement that comes to children in healthy families. As an adult, though, Janie has choices. She can continue to blame her parents for the way they treated her as a child or she can begin acting healthy, rather than reacting to unhealthy people.

———————————

We are influenced by the company we keep. Choose to be with healthy people.

                                            BLB

If people treat you like a doormat, it's because you are lying on the floor.   —JUDY HUEMMER

William sat in group and shared how he avoids conflict at any cost. Rage and physical abuse were common from his father. As an adult William continues to carry an extreme fear of anger. He reports feeling like he "walks on eggshells," and he wonders why people seem to repeatedly take advantage of him.

William treats himself like he's not worth taking care of. He has learned to handle anger passively by keeping it hidden inside and never expressing his feelings.

Our self-esteem grows as we learn to set limits on how others treat us. Anger is not always negative, and it doesn't have to be expressed through rage. We can use anger assertively to set boundaries with others so that they are not allowed to use us or take advantage of us. It takes practice, but we can learn to stand up to others and take care of ourselves through a healthy use of anger.

———————

Assertiveness helps us set boundaries with others and improves our self-esteem.

CSH

> *But now after you have known God, or rather are*
> *known by God, how is it that you turn again to the*
> *weak and beggarly elements, to which you desire*
> *again to be in bondage?*   —GAL. 4:9

Many nights I have lain awake going over events of the day. Thoughts run through my mind about how I could have acted or spoken differently. You've heard those conversations. *If I had only said this instead of what I said. . . . The next time he treats me that way I'm going to do this. . . . Why didn't I speak up? . . . Why didn't I keep my mouth shut?*

Sometimes it seems we have an endless tape running through our head. We can't relax; we can't get to sleep. The harder we try, the more we toss in anguish over the troubles of the day.

Step Ten is important because it teaches us to focus on our program. If we have fallen back into old patterns of worrying, resentment, or anger, we need to ask God to help us to overcome our weaknesses. We can ask God every evening to focus on where we are going rather than on where we have been. We can share our worries and our feelings of resentment with God. As we learn to share and then to let go, serenity is the reward.

Let go and let God (Al-Anon).

BLB

When You said, "Seek My face,"
My heart said to You, "Your face, LORD,
*   I will seek."*
                                    —PS. 27:8

Most of us like to look into the faces of other people. When we have something very difficult to say, though, it is hard for us to look at a person's face. We are afraid of what we will see there. How do we feel when the look we see on someone else's face is *not* the look we want to see? Sometimes we feel inadequate.

There's a big difference when we seek our Lord's face. When we make a mistake and we seek his face, we can know we are forgiven. When we are hurting and we seek his face, we are assured of his comfort. Even when we close our eyes to sleep, we can seek his face and rest in peace. We each need to be aware of whose approving looks we value. The looks of people may disappoint us, but when we seek God's face, we will find acceptance and guidance.

Lord, help others to find love, acceptance, and forgiveness when they look for you in my face.

                                                        CSH

As for me, I will call upon God,
And the Lord shall save me.
Evening and morning and at noon I will
pray, and cry aloud,
And He shall hear my voice.
—PS. 55:16–17

When Mary came to counseling she was full of anger and resentment. She had stuffed over twenty-five years of anger about the way her father had abused her. It was beginning to show in unhealthy ways like isolation from people and addiction to work. She was afraid to express her anger for fear that she would harm herself or someone else.

Through counseling Mary learned three ways to deal with her anger constructively. The first way was to keep a journal of her feelings. She was able to write about things that she could not talk about. The second way was to begin praying about her anger. The third was to release her anger to God little by little.

Anger needs to be released, and finding healthy ways to do this will lead to its proper resolution in your life.

———————————————

Our daily and weekly inventory help us keep our anger healthy and expressed.

BLB

There are defeats more triumphant than victories.
—MONTAIGNE

Janice wept softly. She told the group that she had relapsed the previous night after her fiance broke their engagement. She felt like a failure. For six months she had not binged or purged. Now she believed she would have to start over.

I shared with Janice how I climbed the Statue of Liberty when I was twelve years old. As I climbed the small spiral staircase I panicked, thinking I had somehow started over. Everything continually looked the same.

Relapsing does not mean that we start over. Recovery is often like a spiral staircase. Sometimes as we climb, we keep bumping into the same issue. We have not fallen to the bottom of the steps. We've simply reached a place where we feel like we did at the start of our recovery.

For Janice, the repeated issue was her fear of abandonment. We will all repeatedly face our own major issues as we climb the staircase of recovery. We may feel we lost all of our progress, but if we learn from our defeat, it can become a victory that leads us forward.

Each time I face the same issue, I grow stronger in learning how to handle it.

CSH

*"Watch and pray, lest you enter into temptation.
The spirit truly is ready, but the flesh is weak."*
—MARK 14:38

John comes from a physically abusive family. He and
his brothers were whipped until they bled. His mother
was abused so violently that she had to leave the house
for a month at a time to recover from the beatings.
Many times John's mother would take her sons and go
to her parents' house, only to return to her husband a
month later.

John is struggling today with a desire to rescue his
mother, but he is angry at her for returning time and
again to the abusive environment. He also is struggling
with his obsessive anger at his father. One time his self-
control gave way to a violent battle with his father.
John feels such guilt and shame about that scene that
he continues to keep his feelings bottled up today.

It is important that you take care of unfinished business from childhood. Work through your own "baggage" and become accountable for your strengths and
weaknesses. Learn to live one day at a time. At the end
of that day confess any wrongdoings, ask for forgiveness, and turn it over to God.

Make today the first day of your new life.

BLB

> *The people we relate to need to know we have*
> *boundaries. It will help them and us.*
> —MELODY BEATTIE

Some of us are afraid to say the word *no*. We fear setting boundaries with other people, because they may question the reason for our decision. Whenever we are questioned, we feel a need to appease the other person by explaining every detail. We often give up many of our dreams and goals in saying yes to the desires of others, especially when we want to say no.

Learning to have healthy boundaries requires realizing that we do not have to explain our motivation. If we do not want to do something, then that is the only reason we need to say no. People can learn to respect us, and we can learn to trust ourselves when we start saying what we really mean.

———————

Say what you mean and mean what you say.

CSH

> *For no other foundation can anyone lay than that*
> *which is laid, which is Jesus Christ.*
> —1 COR. 3:11

Education is very important if you want to learn new ways of doing something. If you want to build a boat, you need to learn how. If you want to ride a bicycle, you need to learn how. If you have grown up reacting to stress by drinking or eating and you want to learn a healthier way to cope, you have to learn how.

When Susan wanted to learn a healthy way to raise her children, she got a book on healthy Christian child-raising. As she compared each stage of development to her own childhood, she became painfully aware of how much she had missed out on learning as a child. As she parented her child, she reparented herself to learn new skills in behavior to be used in coping under stress.

———————

Take care of yourself starting today. Start with education. It is never too late to begin again.

BLB

If you aim for nothing, you're sure to hit it.
                              —ANONYMOUS

In the fairy tale *Alice in Wonderland,* Alice has a conversation with the Cheshire cat. Alice asks, "Would you tell me, please, which way I ought to go from here?" "That depends a good deal on where you want to go," replied the cat. "I don't much care where," said Alice. "Then it doesn't matter which way you go," said the cat. This way of thinking may work in Wonderland, but it will not work for those of us who are in recovery.

We will make very little progress if we do not set specific goals for ourselves. Without direction we will continue to wander aimlessly. We need specific plans in order to move forward. For example, it would be too general to decide to try to be a better Christian. It would be more specific to plan to read a devotion each day and to attend a group meeting twice a week.

We can ask God to guide us and give us wisdom to continue to set goals. These goals allow us to continually take inventory of our progress and promptly readjust whenever we get off course.

Continuing to set goals gives us something positive to aim for.
                                                    CSH

> *There are only two lasting gifts parents can leave*
> *youth—one is roots, the other is wings.*
> —ANONYMOUS

A controversy over their eight-year-old son brought Ginny and Scott into my office. Clint was the only child the couple could have, and Ginny was overprotective of him. She refused to let him learn to ride a bike because she feared he might fall and get hurt. She argued that she loved him too much to let him risk injury.

We looked at the difference between loving and rescuing. When we rescue people, we give them a message that they cannot take care of themselves. Continual rescuing leads to emotional retardation, a constant dependence on others to meet all of one's needs.

When we love people, we let go and allow them the freedom to grow up. Maturity comes through painful times. We hate to see our loved ones hurting, but their self-esteem grows when they work through a conflict and realize that they can handle a difficult situation.

In what ways do you rescue others? How can you choose to lovingly let go?

CSH

There is no such thing as something for nothing.
—NAPOLEAN HILL

Bodybuilders spend hours each day working on gaining muscle mass. They set goals and check to see that their progress remains consistent. As they focus on one muscle group, they may do four or five specific exercises with weights. If they work out on a consistent basis, they eventually increase their strength and size.

We would be foolish to think we could develop muscles in only one workout. In the same way, gaining strength in recovery takes dedication to a long process. A brief effort will not produce healthy thinking or behaviors.

Just as bodybuilders schedule their workouts, we need to schedule time to check our progress and take a personal inventory. Only then can we press forward and see the positive results of our recovery.

Daily checks keep us moving toward our goals.

CSH

> *Therefore do not cast away your confidence, which*
> *has great reward. For you have need of endurance,*
> *so that after you have done the will of God, you*
> *may receive the promise.*   —HEB. 10:35–36

Anger is expressed in many ways. We may be angry that we can't change circumstances from being so painful or abusive. We may even be mad at God for allowing things to happen to us.

Some of us are angry at our own behavior. Maybe we spend money we don't have or become so absorbed in work that we shut others out. Maybe we express our anger in an abusive way and then become angry with ourselves. A low self-image causes us to constantly seek approval from others. It backfires on us when we take casual comments as criticism or rejection. The pain we feel causes us to withdraw or to lash out at someone close to us.

God is patient and kind. He loves us no matter what we think or do. He is gentle and he tolerates our immaturity, always guiding us toward self-control.

As we let go of anger inside us, God fills the vacant spots with love.

BLB

"Why make this commotion and weep? The child is not dead, but sleeping. . . . Little girl, I say to you, arise."
                                                              —MARK 5:39, 41

Many of us are unaware that a little child resides within us. It isn't a new or unusual thought. Each one of us started out as a baby and proceeded to live our lives as a little girl or boy. Sometimes children experience tremendous hurt and decide to move prematurely into adulthood. They may think that by doing so they can escape the pain.

As adults we need to realize there is a lovable little child living in us. It is difficult for us to get to know that part of ourselves, because we live in the present. But since God is not on our time schedule and *is* the same yesterday, today, and forever, we can introduce the little child inside to him.

Many of us have never realized that we only experience Jesus as an adult and that the child in us is eager to know him.

Lord, awaken the children within us, and come into their hearts the same way you entered ours.

                                                              CSH

Look to yourselves, that we do not lose those things we worked for, but that we may receive a full reward.
—2 JOHN 1:8

One morning Carol woke up, went into the bathroom to wash her face, and looked into the mirror. What she saw frightened her. She was looking into the face of a stranger. The face was pale with dark circles under the eyes. There was no sparkle of life in them, and her hair was limp, stringy, and dull. Inside she felt just as bad.

Carol is married to an alcoholic. She is as sick from living with an alcoholic as he is from abusing alcohol. Carol has heard about Al-Anon, but she says that her husband needs help, not her.

Carol can find help for herself in the Al-Anon program whether her husband decides to get help for himself or not. In the Al-Anon program you learn what is God's will for your life. You meet others who support and encourage you to take care of yourself. You also learn to accept others and to change yourself. Most important, you learn to forgive yourself for the wrongs you did before you found the miracle of the Twelve-Step program.

———————

Take responsibility for yourself. Be willing to let go of others and let God do his work in them.

BLB

Search out shortcomings and correct them.
—ANONYMOUS

Patsy yelled at her husband for tapping his fingers on the kitchen table. Her anger led them into a fight, and they stopped speaking to each other.

As she sat on the porch and calmed down, Patsy realized that she had overreacted to her husband's noisy little habit. She questioned her anger and realized that her week at work had stressed her and that her allergies had produced a severe headache. Patsy admitted to herself that she blew up over a minor issue.

Once Patsy took responsibility for her anger, she felt free to apologize to her husband. She was sorry for causing their fight, but she felt encouraged at how quickly the problem was resolved.

I can deal with my anger in appropriate ways.

CSH

*For I say, through the grace given to me, to
everyone who is among you, not to think of himself
more highly than he ought to think, but to think
soberly, as God has dealt to each one a measure
of faith.*
                                              —ROM. 12:3

Hazel's parents believed that children were to be
seen and not heard. They also believed that you did
not talk about family problems outside of the family.
Hazel came into counseling because she needed to
change her behavior. She recognized that she was unable to express her feelings constructively because she
had never been allowed to talk about her feelings as a
child. This inability to talk about her problems was
causing problems at work. She was also disappointed
in her relationship with her husband. He was not responding to her in the way she needed him to, but she
did not know how to tell him what she needed.

In therapy we discovered she was still using some of
the behaviors she had learned to use as a child to survive. They worked for her then, but they were not
working for her now that she was an adult. She began
to reparent herself with a new model.

Jesus modeled for us how God wants us to live.

                                              BLB

Good thoughts bear good fruit; bad thoughts bear
bad fruit—and man is his own gardener.
                                            —JOHN LEONARD

The one snowfall of the year was on the day we were trying to leave Dallas for Christmas holidays!

I made a conscious decision not to be upset when our plane was delayed. My husband and I might be late, but we would eventually arrive in Birmingham, as we did. I was proudly explaining to my parents how I had chosen not to get upset, when a voice on the intercom announced that our luggage was still in Dallas.

I had to work on my self-talk over the next two days. I prayed and admitted to God that I had no control over the luggage and that I could now choose how to respond with my feelings. I was inconvenienced, but not angry or depressed.

The program teaches us that we can decide how to feel about any situation that is beyond our control. In the past our habits led us toward depression or anger or into our addictions. These responses did not solve the problem.

As we grow toward health we realize that we can control our self-talk and responses, even when circumstances seem out of our control.

When life feels out of control, I will choose to respond in healthy ways.

                                                            CSH

We have met the enemy, and he is us.
—POGO

One night in group Amanda talked about her difficulty in relationships with men. She is thirty-six and never married, and she wonders if there are "any good men out there." Amanda continues to seek out men who take her on an emotional roller-coaster ride because it feels exciting to her. She allows men to control her feelings of self-worth by whether the relationship is hot or cold.

Amanda receives love and attention the way she received it from her parents. The attention they gave her fluctuated according to their feelings, their opinion of her performance, or how they were treated at work. The group lovingly confronted her on the fact that she was bored with healthy men who offered her a stable kind of love with few ups and downs.

As we learn to respect ourselves, we begin to believe that we deserve respect from others. We accept that we no longer need to tolerate abuse, and we see that a loving relationship is possible.

God's love never jerks us around but always remains stable and consistent. He desires for us to seek relationships based on godly love.

Relationships that reflect God's love may have some ups and downs, but they don't swing to extremes.

CSH

*No temptation has overtaken you except such as is
common to man; but God is faithful, who will not
allow you to be tempted beyond what you are able,
but with the temptation will also make the way of
escape, that you may be able to bear it.*
                                    —1 COR. 10:13

Melissa grew up in an alcoholic home. Many times
her mother told her that she was unwanted. Her
mother drank, was promiscuous with men, and abandoned her from time to time. The only attention Melissa got from her mother was negative and punishing
when Melissa did something wrong. Melissa began recovery by working on separating from her mother.

A few years later Melissa came into group counseling. She wanted attention and the only way she knew
to get it was by being negative. The group confronted
Melissa. They observed that she still gave power to her
mother and let her mother affect her decisions. Her
relationship with her mother was affecting her relationships with other people.

In group, Melissa was able to see patterns in her behavior and to recognize her needs. She was trying to
meet the need she had for love as a child in her relationships with others, but she acted in a negative way
to get others' attention.

———————————

*Through Christ we can experience peace and wholeness by being
vulnerable to our past.*

                                                    BLB

"A new commandment I give to you, that you love one another; as I have loved you, that you also love one another. By this all will know that you are My disciples, if you have love for one another."
—JOHN 13:34–35

Living in the chaos of an alcoholic home, we tend to lash out at others or we isolate ourselves from others. Risking intimate relationships is hard work. Even going to Twelve-Step meetings is threatening, because we are afraid of others seeing us as we really are. But everything requires an element of risk.

Margaret found that happiness is a by-product of giving to others. She volunteered at a children's hospital and began ministering to the parents who were there with their children. She was able to show affection and love to people who were frightened and lonely. She was able to risk reaching out to others and in doing this was able to get in touch with her own feelings.

Our feelings need to be expressed: those of love and empathy as well as those of anger and fear. Friends are there to listen to how we feel, so we need to create time and space for friendships.

The roots of the deepest love die in the heart if not cherished.

BLB

We sought through prayer and meditation to improve our conscious contact with God, as we understood him, praying only for knowledge of his will for us and the power to carry that out.

Alice was really having a hard time with George's drinking. When he came home from work she questioned him about where he had been. She got angry at him whenever she saw him take a drink. He became her enemy, ruining her life by his drinking.

The real enemy is alcoholism. To fight it we need to know what it is. The better you understand the enemy, the easier it is to fight against its power.

Alice prayed that God would heal George spiritually, physically, and emotionally. As the words poured out of her heart, they began to work and the power of alcoholism was defeated. Through prayer Alice found the strength not to be controlled by George's drinking and to love him for who he was.

Love the alcoholic; hate the disease of alcoholism.

FLM

Seek [wisdom] as silver,
And search for [wisdom] as for hidden treasures . . .
—PROV. 2:4

Sometimes we lose contact with people for one reason or another, and the next time we see them we notice how much they've changed. Sadly, the same thing can happen to the relationship between us and our heavenly Father.

Because we can't see God, we tend to forget his presence. Frequently we only think of him when we are in desperate need in a crisis.

The important difference between our earthly relationships and the one we have with God is that he doesn't change every time we talk with him. He is always the same and will always be there when we seek him. Proverbs 2 speaks volumes of the importance of a daily walk and talk with God. It tells how we must search for his knowledge and understanding as we would for something very precious.

Talking to God daily is the only way to let him become our best friend. More importantly, it is the only way we will know his will and recognize his voice when he speaks to us in times of peace or crisis.

CSH

*"He who speaks from himself seeks his own glory;
but He who seeks the glory of the One who sent
Him is true, and no unrighteousness is in Him."*
—JOHN 7:18

Our church put together a cookbook this year. All the members of the church were asked to contribute their favorite recipe. We also have a book that we hand out to visitors. It tells the story of how the women of the church made the tapestry that hangs behind the altar. Both of these books provide us with information.

A third book, the Bible, also provides us with information. When we want to know how to pray, we go to the Psalms and see how David prayed. When we want to know how God expects us to live our lives, we go to Proverbs and see his wisdom. When we want to know how to love Jesus and others, we look at how John loved Jesus and how Jesus loved us.

Knowing where to go to get answers to your questions is important. As Everett George says, "It's in the book."

If you want to know something, ask through prayer and meditation, then go to the Bible for God's answers.

BLB

> *"I tell you the truth. It is to your advantage that I*
> *go away; for if I do not go away, the Helper will*
> *not come to you; but if I depart, I will send Him*
> *to you."*
> —JOHN 16:7

My friend Jeanie Connell recently wrote a song as she was thinking about the picture a child might conjure up from the word *ghost*.

> *You can call him Counselor, You can call him*
> *   Comforter.*
> *You can call him Helper, Advocate, and Spirit of*
> *   Truth.*
>
> *That's the Holy Spirit, better known as "ghost."*
> *He will always be there when you need him most.*
> *Jesus is our brother, God is surely King.*
> *But the Holy Spirit is the reason why I sing.*

There are many times in our lives when we put our trust in a human counselor, rather than the Counselor God designed us to trust.

Counselors are important, but it is also important to remember that only one Counselor is never going to leave us.

CSH

*And do not be conformed to this world, but be
transformed by the renewing of your mind, that you
may prove what is that good and acceptable and
perfect will of God.*
                              —ROM. 12:2

Joni finds it hard to love God because of her perception of him as a rescuer or as a judge. She feels that he
did not rescue her from an abusive father and that God
judges her for being angry at him. She finds it hard to
love others when they have hurt her deeply by verbal
or physical abuse. She has also found it hard to love
herself because she feels that her worth is based on
what she does rather than who she is.

Joni has a beautiful voice and loves to sing and
dance. She would like to do this professionally but she
keeps hearing a voice in the past that said, "You can't
sing; you are not good enough." For all the joy she gets
from singing and for all the joy she brings others who
hear her, she still holds back for fear of not pleasing
that one person who told her she wasn't good enough.
She holds back from serving the Lord because she feels
that she isn't good enough. She holds back from loving
herself because she fears she is not worthy.

God's will for our lives is to love him, love others, and love ourselves.
                                              BLB

"My sheep hear My voice, and I know them, and
they follow Me."
                                              —JOHN 10:27

Sheep develop an intimate relationship with their shepherd. Because of the long hours the shepherd spends with the sheep, they learn the sound of his voice and how to respond to his commands. They are trained to follow where the shepherd leads. The shepherd recognizes his sheep and knows their characteristics.

Jesus desires to be our shepherd so that we can recognize his voice and follow wherever he leads us. In working through the program, we learn to trust his leadership. Members of our group encourage us with experiences of his faithful shepherding abilities. We can draw security from understanding that Jesus knows us personally and chooses the best path for us.

Step Eleven teaches us to improve our contact with God through prayer and meditation. We learn to have an intimate relationship with God by spending time with him.

———————

As we pray for knowledge of his will, God guides us and gives us the strength and power of his plan.

CSH

> *"And now, brethren, I commend you to God and to
> the word of His grace, which is able to build you
> up and give you an inheritance among all those
> who are sanctified."*
>   —ACTS 20:32

When John came to the clinic for counseling, he was struggling about how to meditate on God. The Twelve-Step program offered him a guide. He learned to pray to God each morning, admitting his powerlessness and asking God for the power to make it through the day. Then, as he went through the day, he said that it was a great comfort and help to call on that power to let go of the excess baggage he was carrying around. As he continually turned his life and his will over to God, he received the blessing of power and strength from God.

As we enter into our own meditation with God we need to relax, be consciously aware of what we need to release, and ask God to take this obsession from us. Then we need to let go and let God do his work.

We are each God's children, drawn to him through Christ. Our relationship to Christ rests in our carrying this message to others.

                                                    BLB

> *To everything there is a season,*
> *A time for every purpose under heaven.*
> —ECCL. 3:1

When we read the account of Jesus' lifestyle we see that he was never in a hurry. People were disappointed in Jesus more than once for not getting where they wanted him to be on time. Yet even matters of life and death were not beyond his ability to redeem. In Mark 5 he brought a little girl back to life, and in John 11 he raised Lazarus from the dead.

We all show impatience in different ways. We are not in a hurry for April fifteenth to arrive so we can pay taxes, but we are usually in a hurry to get through the checkout line in the grocery store. We are seldom in a hurry to face the pain of our issues, but we become impatient when recovery seems slow. If we practice adopting the timetable reflected in the life of Jesus, we will learn to slow down and spend time alone with God. We gain patience as we live life one step at a time.

Lord, remind us that you make everything beautiful in its time.

CSH

Put on the whole armor of God, that you may be
able to stand against the wiles of the devil.
                                        —EPH. 6:11

Dick played football in college. During his senior
year he was asked to talk to a grade school football
team about the sport. He began his talk telling them
about how hot it was during summer practice. He said
that just when he was ready to drop the coach would
make him run ten more laps. He also told them about
the sore muscles. By this time the young boys were
looking like they hated football, and the fathers were
wondering why they had invited Dick to talk. Then
Dick told the boys about the glorious feeling he had
when he put on his uniform, buckled the strap of his
helmet, and ran up the ramp at Texas Stadium to the
roar of thirty-five thousand football fans.

Life is like that. We are living the hard times, fighting addictions, trying to salvage a marriage, or trying
not to "fix" others. When we recall whose team we are
on, God renews our strength. We need to put on his
armor and run out onto the field of life.

God's greatest desire is to be glorified, so he renews our strength and
sends us out to show the world his victory.

                                                        BLB

Trying to pray is praying.
—ANONYMOUS

Charlie sat in his bedroom and trembled with nervousness. He wanted to spend time alone with God in prayer, but he was afraid he would somehow pray in the wrong way. With all of his heart, Charlie desired to know God's will for his life, but he felt God might not listen unless he prayed correctly.

Finally Charlie called his sponsor, John, from AA. John explained that prayer means having a conversation with God, and that there is no right or wrong way to pray. John said that the more time he spent in prayer, the more comfortable it became to him.

Charlie hung up the phone and breathed a sigh of relief. It felt good to realize that God did not have expectations for how he should pray. He sat quietly for a while and meditated on his devotional for that day. Then Charlie calmly told God the deep feelings and needs of his heart. He felt peaceful as he left his quiet time, knowing that he had communicated with God.

"For everyone who asks receives, and he who seeks finds, and to him who knocks it will be opened" (Matt. 7:8).

CSH

"Abide in Me, and I in you. As the branch cannot bear fruit of itself, unless it abides in the vine, neither can you, unless you abide in Me."
—JOHN 15:4

Sometimes we go to God to tell him the thoughts we have and what rests heavy on our hearts. Other times, we just need to be in God's presence. We need to feel his power, feel his presence, and rest in his love. There are times when we desperately need God to talk to us. We cry out for his voice to tell us what to do. Whether talking with God, being with God, or listening for God's words, we need this time of meditation daily.

Sarah has conversations with God all day long. As she drives to work she talks to him, during the day she asks his guidance, and in the evening she prays to him before she goes to sleep. She is steadfast in her prayer life, patient in her waiting, and open to the words of the Lord.

As we go to the Lord in prayer, asking for our needs to be met and seeking his guidance, let us remember to acknowledge his power and praise him for his blessings.

BLB

> *"Ask, and it will be given to you; seek, and you will find; knock, and it will be opened to you."*
>
> —MATT. 7:7

Before Muriel entered recovery she avoided solitude. She only felt safe if there were other people around to distract her from the pain of loneliness. Whenever she was alone, Muriel panicked.

Now that she has focused on working the steps, Muriel is learning to enjoy quiet times. Each morning she sets aside a time of solitude to talk with God and to listen for answers to her questions. This special time of prayer, meditation, and reflection help to start her day with God in control as her Higher Power.

Each evening Muriel stops again to review the day. She checks to see if there are areas in her life that need improvement. Then she remembers the things she did well and pauses to enjoy them. This evening time helps her regain serenity; the stress and tensions of the day flow away as she gives them to God.

Meditation is a time of healing.

CSH

> *Evening and morning and at noon*
> *I will pray, and cry aloud,*
> *And He shall hear my voice.*
> —PS. 55:17

When we get physically sick we call the doctor for a prescription. The doctor gives us the latest miracle drug and tells us to get plenty of rest and drink a lot of fluids. The same routine is healing for spiritual illness. The miracle prescription is confession and repentance. Then we are to rest in the Lord, while taking in his words.

Six steps to filling our soul spiritually are:

1. Go to a place where you can be alone with the Lord.

2. Schedule your time so that it won't always be at the end of the day when you are tired.

3. Be open and honest in telling God your thoughts and feelings.

4. Take the time to listen carefully to God's answers.

5. Meditate on his words.

6. End your time with the Lord by saying, "Your will, not mine, be done."

Are you spending more time talking to God and less time listening to his answers?

BLB

And in His law he meditates
 day and night.
He shall be like a tree
Planted by the rivers of water.
                    —PS. 1:2–3

David wrote in Psalm 1 about the benefits of setting our mind on God's Word. God's Word gives us clear direction to become like the tree David describes in this verse. We need a set standard to guide us down a path, and God's Word can provide that for us.

David says if we meditate on and delight in God's Word, we are like a strong tree firmly planted by a stream of water. Just as the tree remains stable, we become stable and solid in our faith. We draw spiritual nourishment through trusting in God's unconditional love, realizing that he is faithful, and accepting his forgiveness of our past.

A tree planted and growing in a healthy environment produces fruit. The fruit for us will be a closer spiritual relationship with God, a healthier view of our own value, and the ability to share our experiences to encourage other people in the program.

Our growth depends on the nourishment and environment with which we surround ourselves.

                                                    CSH

Blessed is the man
Who walks not in the counsel of the ungodly,
Nor stands in the path of sinners,
Nor sits in the seat of the scornful;
But his delight is in the law of the LORD,
And in His law he meditates day and night.
                                    —PS. 1:1–2

Working the Twelve-Step program gives us the opportunity to change our own self-defeating behavior. To make these changes we all need support, which often comes in the form of words—words from our friends in the program as they speak their feelings from the heart, words from our sponsors as they confront us in our relapses and guide us in our progress, words from our Lord as he tells us how to live our life.

The words of our Lord tell us to enter by the narrow gate and follow him. As we do so, we see the spiritual path ahead that leads us away from self-defeating behavior and toward a life directed by Christ.

The Twelve-Step program is our key to opening the gate. Once opened, the Lord leads us down the path ahead.

                                              BLB

> *But the fruit of the Spirit is love, joy, peace,*
> *longsuffering, kindness, goodness, faithfulness,*
> *gentleness, self-control.* —GAL. 5:22–23

An apple orchard is a lovely place to spend a spring afternoon. If we could set up camp in the orchard and watch the apples grow, we would never hear the trees moaning as they forced themselves to produce apples. Growing apples is the natural function of an apple tree and is not painful to the tree.

God has given us a list of the fruit he desires to produce in our lives. We have longed for joy in living, peace during struggles, longsuffering toward others, and self-control. These are a few of the valuable fruits God will allow to grow in us.

We sometimes worry that we will have to work really hard and strain ourselves to produce spiritual fruit. Just like the apple tree, we can relax and let the production of fruit in our lives be a natural result of our being God's children. As we spend time meditating on God's word and praying, God will produce spiritual fruit in each of us.

God desires for us to spend time with him and then to relax and know he is in control.

CSH

For whatever is born of God overcomes the world.
And this is the victory that has overcome the
world—our faith.   —1 JOHN 5:4

How do you forget the pain of being physically abused as a child? How do you erase from your memory the embarrassment of a drunk parent showing up at your basketball game?

Children are vulnerable. Children can be the most caring individuals in the world; they can love unconditionally. The faith of a child is very trusting. They have to learn to distrust.

If we could go back to our childhoods, we would be vulnerable in our unconditional love, open to new experiences, and loving of everyone. We could again face the possibility of painful experiences that lead to distrust. Still, the promise is that if we belong to God we can become childlike again through faith. We can focus on the love promised to us in the future and forget, with God's help, the pain of the past.

If we don't move forward, then we are moving backward.

BLB

"Beware, lest you forget the LORD."
—DEUT. 6:12

We all know people who get a prescription that clearly says to take a medication for two weeks, yet when they begin to feel better, they stop taking the medication. They wonder why their illness returns so quickly. Could it be because they did not follow the directions?

As we continue in the process of recovery, we will have times that feel peaceful. We admitted the nature of our wrongs. We asked God to remove our shortcomings. We even sought to make amends with the people we harmed. The peace that comes through working the steps is a delightful place of healing. Good times, though, can be dangerous.

We can become so comfortable feeling life is now manageable that we give God little or no place in our thoughts. This can lead to complacency.

We must be careful to never forget the source of our blessings. The truth is that we are still powerless apart from our Higher Power. If we forget to receive our power from God, our lives can easily become unmanageable again.

————————

Even in the good times, God is our Higher Power. We must seek through prayer and meditation to follow his will for our lives.

CSH

*Let the word of Christ dwell in you richly in all
wisdom, teaching and admonishing one another in
psalms and hymns and spiritual songs, singing with
grace in your hearts to the Lord.*   —COL. 3:16

As Jane worked the Twelve Steps, she made contact
with God in ways that progressively became more intimate and meaningful. In Step Three she turned her life
and her will over to God. In Step Five she laid her sins
at Jesus' feet. As she worked on through the program,
she asked God in Step Seven to make her aware of
things she needed to work on.

Jane keeps a journal and occasionally she reads her
writings from the past to see just how far she has
grown spiritually and emotionally. Today she asks God
to give her the wisdom and strength to continue growing spiritually and emotionally. She can see from her
journal writings that he has opened her eyes to see
new things every day that help her to grow. This is a
spiritual awakening that she has achieved through
prayer and daily meditation.

*When we record in a journal our prayers and the answers God gives
us, we become ever more mindful of his presence in our lives.*

BLB

*The love of God was manifested toward us, that
God has sent His only begotten Son into the world,
that we might live through Him.*

—1 JOHN 4:9

I remember a time in elementary school when I noticed a cute blonde-headed boy on the playground. It was the first time that I felt the tug in my heart known as "puppy love." Plucking the petals from a daisy one by one, I would say to myself, "He loves me, he loves me not." When the last petal of the daisy ended on "He loves me not," I felt terribly hurt and disappointed.

Some of us tend to use the daisy method to determine whether or not God loves us. If life is taking a positive turn, then we believe we are loved by God. If we struggle through a difficult time, we may feel abandoned and unloved by God.

We need to realize that during hard times we often base our beliefs on feelings instead of facts. God's love for us remains at the same constant level, even when we may not feel loved.

A reliable way of knowing God loves us is by meditating on all he does for us. He gave his very life to save us from our sin! We can be sure that God's love is unfailing because he has proven it beyond a doubt.

We can be confident that God loves each person intimately.

CSH

Whom He predestined, these He also called; whom
He called, these He also justified; and whom He
justified, these He also glorified. What then shall
we say to these things? If God is for us, who can
be against us?   —ROM. 8:30–31

Dorothy found that the first step for success in the Twelve-Step program was prayer. She sought the power of God in her life to become sober and to maintain her sobriety. With God's help she has remained sober for fourteen years.

After praying for God's power, Dorothy had to take a hard look at herself. She had to let go of a lot of remembrances of the past. She needed to change a lot of behavior. She also needed to learn healthier ways of thinking and feeling in the future.

Praying and changing her behavior were the first two aspects of success in Dorothy's program. Next she set up a time of daily meditation. This was her quiet time each day when she could sit and reflect on what the Lord had to say to her.

God can give us the peace to go forth into the day if we begin each day in prayer, open ourselves to change, and meditate on his Word.

BLB

God shall supply all your need according to His
riches in glory by Christ Jesus.   —PHIL. 4:19

In the late 1800s a woman was traveling with her four-year-old son on a train. She had brought along the boy's nanny to take care of him. At one point, the boy began to fuss and cry. The mother was annoyed and questioned why the child was upset. The nanny responded, "He is crying because I wouldn't let him have something that he wanted." "Give him whatever he wants and keep him quiet," replied the mother.

Several moments passed, and suddenly the boy screamed in pain. Angrily the mother yelled, "I told you to give him whatever he wants." "I did," replied the nanny. "He wanted a wasp."

We are often like this child. We see something or someone we want, and we beg God to let us have it. It is difficult for us to understand that God is not trying to deprive us when he tells us no.

God sees the big picture. He knows that if we received some of our desires we would find a sting of pain. Because he loves us he withholds some of the things we desire. He is wise enough to know what we really need.

—————————

We can trust that God always has our best interest in mind.

CSH

*The things which you learned and received and
heard and saw in me, these do, and the God of
peace will be with you.*   —PHIL. 4:9

My mother grew up with an imaginary little boy
named Bright. On Sundays she and her sisters would
walk the three blocks to the church. That was where
she loved to sing about Bright.

Every Sunday morning the congregation and the
choir would sing out all the good old songs. My
mother's favorite was the song, "Brighten the Corner
Where You Are." My mother would look around as she
sang, wondering where Bright was and why he was
always in the corner. As she got older she realized that
each of us is Bright. We each can brighten the corner
where we are.

*Next time you sing in church, brighten up; someone may need the
beam from your light.*

BLB

Accepting my limitations with a humble spirit saves me time, pain, and energy.
                                    —DWIGHT WOLTER

On a playground children sit on opposite ends of a seesaw and ride up and down. This game works out well when both children are approximately the same size, but if an adult and a child ride the seesaw the game can become out of balance. The larger person can use his weight to control the game. Having the game out of balance may frustrate the child to the point that he dislikes riding a seesaw.

Many of us grew up in homes where nothing was in balance. Everything seemed extreme, desperate, and dramatic. We knew nothing of calm, and balance seemed boring. Some of us carried this into adulthood and found new ways to create chaos and avoid boredom.

Most of our imbalance is an attempt to control our surroundings. The prayer and meditation of the Eleventh Step can help restore balance to our lives.

When we meditate on God's Word, he can keep our feelings and actions in balance.

                                                        CSH

"Assuredly, I say to you, if you have faith and do not doubt, you will not only do what was done to the fig tree, but also if you say to this mountain, 'Be removed and be cast into the sea,' it will be done. And all things, whatever you ask in prayer, believing, you will receive."

—MATT. 21:21–22

Barbara constantly asks questions rather than talking in a more sharing way. She begins the conversation asking about your family, your job, and your activities. One question leads to another as she continues to follow up each answer you give with another question. You feel overwhelmed and exhausted trying to supply the information and then you feel angry that she is so inquisitive and probing.

We sometimes talk this way with our children. We ask too many questions rather than just being available to them in an open and nonjudgmental way. When we quiz or criticize, they become defensive and quit talking.

At times we all are like this. But we have God as a model of how to listen and Jesus as a model of how to speak in a loving, caring way.

Speak openly and honestly about what you think and feel in a loving and caring way.

BLB

"I have come as a light into the world, that
whoever believes in Me should not abide in
darkness."
                                        —JOHN 12:46

During a thunderstorm one night the lights went off in Michal's home. For years she had kept a flashlight in a drawer of her bedside table to use in emergencies. Michal found the flashlight and switched it on, but nothing happened. Over the years the batteries had lost their power. All of the components of the flashlight were operable, but because there was no energy in the batteries, the flashlight could not produce light.

Before we have a personal relationship with Jesus Christ, we are like a flashlight with no batteries. We have no light within and are unable to see the path toward God.

When we receive Christ in our hearts, he becomes the energy source that produces light in us. Our purpose is to shine, but we can only do that with God as the source of power in our lives. His light will illumine the path ahead of us and guide us to truth.

We no longer need to fear the darkness when we walk in God's light.
                                                        CSH

> *Be anxious for nothing, but in everything by prayer*
> *and supplication, with thanksgiving, let your*
> *requests be made known to God; and the peace of*
> *God, which surpasses all understanding, will guard*
> *your hearts and minds through Christ Jesus.*
> —PHIL. 4:6–7

We have basic needs in life: the need for food, water, and shelter, the need for love, and the need for self-fulfillment. Gloria grew up in an alcoholic home and did not have these needs met. There was never a meal on the table. Her family scrounged for their food. When she had a serious kidney infection, the welfare department stepped in and took her to the clinic for treatment. There was no love for her or her five sisters. The father valued only boys; he abused his girls.

Children need food, water, and safety and find ways of getting these needs met by screaming and crying. As adults they learn to deaden their pain with alcohol, drugs, food, sex, and even work. In many instances needy people attract each other when other sources of love are absent.

We ask God to help us accept our past, since we cannot change it. Then we ask him for courage to change ourselves. He will help us reach out to healthy sources that will meet our needs.

With God's help we can heal the past and risk reaching out to the future.

BLB

Satan wants to see perfection. God wants to see improvement.
—CHRIS THURMAN

All of us have picked up negative messages from the past. Some of us were so good at hearing negative messages that we began to see the Bible as a book of legalism and conditional love.

God gave us helpful guidelines for life, but he also gave realistic passages about human weakness, our need for rest, and how to have peace of mind. The rules were intended to motivate the lazy. The verses of peace, rest, and comfort were given to ease the burden of the perfectionist and the overachiever. To read only one message will give us an extreme view of God and increase our dysfunction.

Our church recently featured a motivational speaker who enthusiastically told us what we "need," "should," and "ought" to do to have success and spiritual growth. Before recovery I would have felt guilty for not living up to such lofty expectations. Today I am learning to assess where I am already performing adequately, where I need improvement, and where I choose not to compete at all. Since no amount of performance can generate love from others anyway, I can lift the pressures and just be myself.

Today I can accept my limitations as graciously as God does and love myself in spite of them.

CSH

> *But we have this treasure in earthen vessels, that*
> *the excellence of the power may be of God and*
> *not of us.*
> —2 COR. 4:7

We are like pieces of pottery molded by the hands of God into different shapes and sizes. We are fragile clay shells, vessels that can be broken.

But it is said that we have a treasure. What is it? This splendid treasure is the gospel that we carry in our clay pots. It fills us and gives us strength.

If the light of the gospel shines within us, it can shed power and wisdom on all we do. However, if we don't have a crack or two in our clay forms, the light of the gospel cannot shine forth so others can see it.

We all have rough edges here and there, reminders of the challenges we've met. Our vessels crack and break when we experience pain and suffering. But with the Word of God supporting our frame, and his unconditional love and promises coursing through our veins, we will be sustained. We will shine as examples to others.

God uses cracked pots to show us the powers of his healing love as it shines through the cracks.

FLM

*Now the Lord is the Spirit; and where the Spirit
of the Lord is, there is liberty. But we all, with
unveiled face, beholding as in a mirror the glory
of the Lord, are being transformed into the same
image from glory to glory, just as by the Spirit of
the Lord.*
                              —2 COR. 3:17–18

An art teacher once taught me how to wash my canvas with paint and then pick out shapes and colors from the design the wash made on the canvas. Last night I was reminded of that art lesson as I was driving from Albuquerque to Santa Fe at sunset. In front of me were majestic mountains capped with snow. The clouds swirled above the mountains with colors of pink, gray, and white floating above the purple, green, and charcoal peaks. Behind me in the rearview mirror was the sunset. The sky looked like a giant orange fire, ablaze with streaks shooting out in every direction. The lighter areas were yellow and red; the darker areas, deep rust and burnt orange. It was magnificent.

We can see life the same way if we look through the eyes of our Creator.

———————————

God makes all things in a myriad of shapes and colors.

                                        BLB

*Having had a spiritual awakening as the result of
these steps, we tried to carry this message to others
and to practice these principles in all our affairs.*

We should all be "respondible" to others. No, that is
not a misspelled word. Responsible is another trait. We
need to think about "respondibility." The Good Samaritan showed "respondibility." When he saw someone in
need, he stopped and helped. In Step Twelve, we are
encouraged to respond to those around us. We need to
share with them the power that is great enough to free
us from our self-will, the power that can help us see our
strengths and weaknesses, the power that can forgive
and lead us to forgiveness of ourself and others.

God responds to us and empowers us to respond to
others. That is what "respondibility" is. It means looking around us and being aware of who has fallen and
needs a steadying hand. As the miracle of the program
works in us, we are compelled to respond by sharing
this miracle of healing with others. As Good Samari-
tans we need to stop, look around, and extend our
hand of love and kindness to those in need.

The price we pay is the cost of the gift we have received.

BLB

When the heart is right, feet are swift.
—THOMAS JEFFERSON

Few of us are able to recall information concerning people from the past, such as who was the Secretary of State ten years ago or who won the Heisman Trophy five years ago. Although we were interested in this news at the time, we quickly forgot these people because they never directly influenced our lives. We remember those who have touched our lives.

In working the Twelve-Step program we have received grace and acceptance from others. People who were further along guided and supported us in recovery. They listened to our "immoral inventory" and loved us unconditionally.

Stop for a moment and call to mind the names and faces of those people who demonstrated God's grace to you. Those dear people are the ones who are easy to remember. Once our hearts have been captured by God's acceptance and healing graciousness toward us, we can demonstrate and offer grace to others in the program.

_____

We seek to carry this message of freedom to others and to practice these principles in all our affairs.

CSH

"Go home to your friends, and tell them what great things the Lord has done for you, and how He has had compassion on you."   —MARK 5:19

The question we all have when we first enter a Twelve-Step program is, "Why am I here?" We would rather blame the other person for our problems.

As I worked through the steps, turning my life and will over to God, taking a real look at my own behavior and attitudes, mending the fences of my relationships, and then reaching out to others, I had a quickening of the Spirit within me. Suddenly I was grateful to be where I was. The Twelve-Step program of Al-Anon was a very powerful influence in my life. It opened me to healing, forgiveness, and love. Through the program I found relief from the pain of resentment and anger. When I felt the forgiveness of God for all the wrongs I had done, I was then open to forgiving others. With anger gone, I was able to open up to love.

I am a grateful member of Al-Anon. Without this spiritually healing Twelve-Step program, I would be lonely, angry, and living in darkness. Today there is the light of the Lord in my life.

With the help of the Lord I will practice the principles of the Twelve-Step program in my daily life.

BLB

May the God of all grace, . . . after you have
suffered a while, perfect, establish, strengthen,
and settle you.   —1 PETER 5:10

One of the blessings we receive by sharing in the Twelve-Step program is seeing a reflection of vulnerability from the person with whom we share our walk. The more we share the truth of our spiritual journey, the stronger we become.

When we go to our support groups, we are accepted and loved right where we are at any given moment. We gain wisdom as the members share their joys, sorrows, progress, and fears. We feel affirmed, inspired, thankful, and strengthened to face another day.

Once we were needy, but now we can reach out to others who are in need. Because we are now restored to a healthy spiritual and emotional balance, we can lead others into the way of restoration. In the same way God used people in the program to nurture us, we can now offer gentle guidance to those who are just beginning the journey of recovery.

We must pass our knowledge on to others in order to continue our recovery.

CSH

> *Brethren, if a man is overtaken in any trespass, you*
> *who are spiritual restore such a one in a spirit of*
> *gentleness, considering yourself lest you also be*
> *tempted.*
> —GAL. 6:1

Circles can be very symbolic in our lives. They can refer to family circles, our circle of friends, the circle of the Earth, and the circle many of our lives take. I've always wondered why we sat in circles as children. Then as we became teenagers, it was extremely important that we ran with the right circle of friends. Usually the older we became, the wider our circles grew.

John got caught in a circle of addiction. He drank to escape the pain of his low self-image. The more he drank, the worse he felt about himself and the more he needed to drink to escape the pain of his feelings. Finally his circle spun out of control and he lost all connection with others.

And then a new circle began. He attended a Twelve-Step program and sat around a table in a circle. He began to connect with others and have a circle of friends. He began to feel connected with God and had a spiritual awakening.

Next time you feel out of control, reach out and form a circle with God and with those he sends your way.

BLB

We love Him because He first loved us.
—1 JOHN 4:19

Because Jenny was an incest victim she had a hard time seeing God as a loving, caring, or protecting Father. She remembered the pain and fear of being alone with no one to call to for protection. Jenny wondered where God was and why he didn't intervene and protect her. What was wrong with her that God didn't love her as much as he loved others?

We often fail to realize that God understands why we do not see him as a loving Father. Our view of God's love is marred by the evil done to us by perpetrators who were supposed to be our role models. God wants us to understand that he was there when we were abused and that he grieved with us when we were victimized. He hated the evil done to us so much that he allowed his Son Jesus to die for that evil.

God can and does heal our hurt. God uses the pain of abuse to help us understand the great love he has for us. We can share his love with others who are hurting.

Spending time with God opens our ears and our hearts to our own needs and to the needs of others.

CSH

*And let us consider one another in order to stir up
love and good works, not forsaking the assembling
of ourselves together, as is the manner of some, but
exhorting one another, and so much the more as
you see the Day approaching.*

—HEB. 10:24–25

To grow up in a home where there is alcoholism is
unhealthy. People from these homes grow up hurting
and need to know about Al-Anon or one of the other
Twelve-Step programs. Some of the symptoms of an
unhealthy family are drug abuse, perfectionism, gam-
bling, compulsive overeating, and compulsive shopping.

Pat had a problem with compulsive overeating. She
met Judy who had the same problem. They began calling each other and helping each other combat the urge
to binge on food. Pat was helped by a group called
Overeaters Anonymous, and she sponsored Judy in the
same program. The program was based on the same
Twelve Steps as Alcoholics Anonymous. Helping
others is called Twelve Stepping.

When we share our struggles with compulsive behavior or addictions with another who has the same
problem, we help them and ourselves.

What I give is never as much as what I receive from giving.

BLB

*And we know that all things work together for
good to those who love God.*   —ROM. 8:28

Jeanie intended to share her personal story of child
sexual abuse with a group of middle-school youths.
The night before she spoke, Jeanie washed some
clothes. When she took the clothes out of the dryer, the
entire load (including her favorite shirt) looked as if it
had been sprayed with purple paint. After she removed all of the clothing, she found the wrapper from
a purple crayon. The crayon had disappeared; only the
wrapper remained.

The following day Jeanie shared how, as a child, she
felt ashamed and embarrassed about being touched by
someone she thought she could trust. She could smile
and make people believe she was happy, so she decided to keep her feelings hidden inside. As an adult
suffering from depression and eating disorders, she
learned that what seemed like one small thing in the
past had actually touched every area of her life. God
used the perfect "visual aid." Jeanie held up her favorite shirt, now splashed with purple, as a reminder of
the damage even one hurtful secret can do.

———————————

*Lord, use my difficult, painful places to help others and bring
you glory.*

CSH

Therefore, since we have this ministry, as we have received mercy, we do not lose heart.
                                        —2 COR. 4:1

One night five years ago my mother fell and suffered multiple injuries. While she was in the emergency room I prayed that God would give her the strength to survive and that he would give the doctors wisdom to treat her effectively. Through the mercy of the Lord she survived, and today I have the ministry of caring for her.

She did not ask much of me before her accident. She was pretty independent, always sacrificing for her family. Today I am able to give of my time to her. I receive strength to minister to her when I remember the words of Paul and know that the Lord strengthens those who serve him.

Having had a spiritual awakening, then Christ desires us to go to others and minister to them. Except for the mercy of God in our own lives, we would not be called to carry the message to others.

                                                    BLB

That you may become blameless and harmless, children of God without fault . . . you shine as lights in the world.
                              —PHIL. 2:15

Children love lights! They are especially drawn to Christmas lights, fireflies, and flashlights. God's Word says a lot about light.

Can we each imagine a large spotlight shining on our life? Where would we want it to focus? Sometimes we wish the spotlight would shine directly on us to highlight our abilities and talents for everyone to see.

What would our life be like if our only desire were to focus on God in us? We would probably want the spotlight to point others to God as a source of strength and not to us. That doesn't mean that we are not to help others, but the greatest support we can offer anyone is to help lead them out of darkness by introducing them to "the light of the world"—Jesus.

God, let everything in our lives become a mere shadow in the light of you.

                                        CSH

*May the Lord make you increase and abound in
love to one another and to all, just as we do to you.*
—1 THESS. 3:12

When John came out of treatment he was so thankful
for his new life that he wanted to rush out and save
others from the disease of alcoholism. Of course, no
one was sitting around waiting for him to haul them off
to treatment. From his own experience John knew to
go slowly and just be there for others when they
needed him. Sometimes the cry for help comes to him
in the form of a phone call late at night. Other times it's
over lunch, when a buddy asks him about his experience in the treatment center. Others have asked him if
he misses drinking and he always says, "No, I have
found too many wonderful things in sobriety."

John serves the Lord faithfully by his presence
weekly at church services, by his gifts to the church,
by his prayers, and by his service on church commit-
tees. John does not have time to be tempted to drink.
He is busy walking with the Lord and doing whatever
the Lord asks him to do.

---

*As we go about the Lord's business, he gives us the strength to battle
temptation.*

FLM

> *Though the soul is healed, God still sees the*
> *wounds, and sees them not as scars, but as*
> *honours.*   —JULIAN OF NORWICH

One of the twelve AA promises says, "We will not regret the past nor wish to shut the door on it." So often we look back with regret for wasted years, for wrongs done to us, and for wrongs done by us.

God does not see them as such. Each experience provides a stepping-stone toward God. Whether in pursuit of the god of religion, money, fame, or sex, each has brought us to a blockade. If we retreat to pursue a new path toward the true God, it has then proved profitable because God wants to love us and to imprint with his grace. By seeing how failures bring about growth, we can learn to appreciate them. We can more freely receive God's forgiveness and, in turn, offer it to others.

It has been said that mental health is the ability to accept failure and pursue life anyway. The Twelve Steps help us toward that goal.

Today I can accept my failures and offer them as markers for other travelers.

CSH

*Let us consider one another in order to stir up love
and good works, not forsaking the assembling of
ourselves together, as is the manner of some.*
                                        —HEB. 10:24–25a

When David went through treatment for alcoholism
he was introduced to the Twelve-Step program of Alcoholics Anonymous. He attended a meeting and felt this
was a group of people who not only cared about his
recovery, but also offered him a guide to follow. The
first requirement was that he attend ninety meetings
in ninety days. This seemed like a time-consuming activity, but as he began attending meetings he began to
depend on the support that the group offered.

Many months later he found himself welcoming people into the program and advising them to attend
ninety meetings in ninety days.

The program is designed for us to love and be with
each other. As we assemble we form a circle of
strength with the power of God in the center. The circle is never broken. Instead, as we reach out and touch
others, they are brought into the circle. The circle continually grows and increases in love and good works.

Two can begin a circle and thousands can be touched.

                                        FLM

> *To live means sharing one another's space, dreams,*
> *sorrows, contributing our ears to hear, our eyes to*
> *see, our arms to hold, our hearts to love.*
> —PAUL TILLICH

All of us have a message worth sharing, regardless of how far we've come or how far we have to go. If we can't share what does work, we can surely share what doesn't. Both are helpful.

Sharing in a safe place builds trust. My message is not the same as yours. In sharing, we get both perspectives.

New opportunities and challenges surface as we share. Gradually we gain confidence to risk new behaviors. With practice we get more comfortable with these changes. The more comfortable we become, the more likely we will be to share with others. This is the success of Twelve-Step programs—a willing sharing with others, both inside and outside the group.

Share your story with another, for you have much to give.

CSH

> *Those who wait on the LORD*
> *Shall renew their strength;*
> *They shall mount up with wings like eagles;*
> *They shall run and not be weary,*
> *They shall walk and not faint.*
>
> —ISA. 40:31

God, I'm busy again. I'm cleaning out my closets and packing in a frenzy. I'm determined to make this move to a new city in a fresh way. I want to break my old defeating habits and begin new clean ones. But I'm having a problem, Lord. All my willpower seems to be poured out on the earth as if it had never been. When my will is aligned with yours, it becomes mighty; but today I feel tired, weak, and in despair.

How tragic that we trust our own strength, when what we crave is the chance to begin again, knowing from the wisdom of all our scars what not to do. God, serenity is simple when I take time to allow you to reveal yourself, to perceive your will, and then to flow with it.

Help me remember that you are the source of all new life. You give me not one or three or seven new chances, but as many as I need, drawing me ever nearer to you.

_____

God gives us the gift of strength in despair, forgiveness in failure, energy when tired, and newness when needed (Kit Fensterbush).

BLB

To them God willed to make known what are the riches of the glory . . . which is Christ in you, the hope of glory.
                                                —COL. 1:27

Many of us have lived life according to our emotions. We can learn to celebrate our past when we are able to separate it from our feelings.

We celebrate the past as a part of who we are, a part of God's creation. We can celebrate it now because we understand that, though our plans can be destroyed or delayed, God's purposes cannot! God continues to move forward in our lives, using our detours and mistakes to accomplish his will.

Through the pain of memories and feelings we reach out to God, the Father we always longed for. Every time we share our journey of recovery with other people who are hurting, we can celebrate. We know that God has helped us face what was too painful to speak about and now uses our victory to minister to others.

We don't celebrate because we no longer have feelings that sometimes hurt or because we never feel angry. We celebrate because we know that with God we are always cared for, in spite of our circumstances.

Since God can make something beautiful out of the past, imagine what he will do with the present.

                                                CSH

Oh, give thanks to the LORD! . . .
Sing to Him; . . .
Talk of all His wondrous works.
　　　　　—PS. 105:1–2

Picture a sunny day. You're driving down the street with windows down and music blasting over the radio, and you're singing away. You pull up to a stoplight, casually glance over, and see a carload of hysterical teenagers. And there you are, stuck at perhaps the longest red light in history. So you sit there, slinking under the steering wheel in your embarrassment.

For me, this is an everyday occurrence. However, there is one song I hope people catch me singing: "From a Distance," arranged by Arif Mardin and Steve Skinner and recorded by Bette Midler. Actually I look for people to pull up next to, and I turn the volume up. "From a distance, we are instruments marching in our common band, playing songs of hope, playing songs of peace. They're the songs of every man. God is watching us from a distance."

Usually people look over at me, chuckle, and drive on. I won't get a chance to tell them how I feel about God. Perhaps, though, they'll tell someone about the woman bellowing that song, and maybe they'll remember the words, "God is watching us."

Make a joyful noise and sing!

BLB

Jesus Christ is the same yesterday, today,
and forever.   —HEB. 13:8

Understanding the concept of God's unconditional love for us is often difficult. Many of us feel unworthy of such overwhelming acceptance from God. We often feel guilty for our past failures, so we compose a mental list of all the things we have done wrong and then decide that God could never love someone as "lousy" as we are. Others of us who feel unworthy try to gain God's love through performance. We believe that if we work hard enough, that will make us good enough to receive the love of God.

The truth is that God's love does not have anything to do with us, but it has *everything* to do with God. He loves us because it is an attribute of his character to express unconditional love toward us.

The verse for today assures us that the love of God will never change. God will never love us any more or any less than he does at this very moment! What will change is our love and dedication for God. As we seek to know him and spend time learning the truths that the Bible has to offer, we will grow into a richer, fuller, and more intimate relationship with God.

There is nothing that can ever separate us from the love of God.
                                                    CSH

Show me Your ways, O LORD;
Teach me Your paths.
Lead me in Your truth and teach me,
For You are the God of my salvation;
On You I wait all the day.
                    —PS. 25:4–5

Working the Twelve-Step program becomes a way of life. As we work through each step, that step becomes an integral part of our behavior, beliefs, and speech. You cannot turn your life over to God, asking him to mold you and use you in doing his will, without there being a noticeable influence on your behavior and words. Nor can you unpack the baggage you have been carrying around for years without your appearance changing. No longer are you weighted down with anger, fear, greed, and bitterness. You walk tall, shoulders relieved of their heavy burden. As you continue working the steps, Christ lives in you, and his presence guides you to lead others who are still struggling.

Being a sponsor to someone in the program is a great honor. As we sponsor we need to remember to offer only support, to share our experiences in using the program, and to model for them the hope of recovery.

Hope, support, and experience: these are the three hands of friendship that we offer to those who come to the program.

BLB

"No one, when he has lit a lamp, covers it . . . , but sets it on a lampstand, that those who enter may see the light."
　　　　　　　　　　　　　　　　　　—LUKE 8:16

Wendy and her husband Jack were camping out for their yearly vacation. The night grew dark, and Jack lit the lantern to provide light.

When Wendy began to fumble through her backpack, Jack placed a bucket over the lantern. "What are you doing?" Wendy exclaimed. "I can't see anything!" "The light is still on," Jack said calmly. "Of course the lantern is on, but you covered it up," responded Wendy.

Jack uncovered the light and explained his reason for hiding it. He told Wendy that he was proud of all her hard work in her Twelve-Step group. His concern was that, although she had learned a lot about recovery and had "light" to share, she was hiding it from others. Wendy said that she felt timid but she was determined to start sharing her recovery with others as soon as they returned home.

Let your light shine brightly on the lives of others.

CSH

*Then Jesus said to His disciples, "If anyone desires
to come after Me, let him deny himself, and take up
his cross, and follow Me."*   —MATT. 16:24

Several years ago while on vacation in Santa Fe, I was
looking for something to buy as a souvenir. I walked in
front of the Governor's Palace where the local Native
Americans sell their wares and I spotted a beautiful
little silver cross. It had a design etched in the silver by
one of the native craftspeople. I bought the cross, hung
it on a silver chain, and have worn it around my neck
every day since my trip.

This morning I was hurrying to get ready for work.
Just as I put my dress on, the chain holding the cross
came undone and both the chain and the cross fell on
the floor. My first reaction was to pick both up, put
them on the dresser, rush through dressing, and get
going. But then I stopped and thought, *How often are
we tempted to cast the cross aside because we are too
busy or too rushed?* I stopped, picked up the cross, put
it back on the chain, and hung it securely around my
neck.

---

*The Power that comes from the Cross is the Power that strengthens us
to carry our burdens.*

BLB

*Following our feelings usually leads us down the
wrong path.*
                                        —MICHAL SPELL

Diane sat on the hillside and ran her fingers through
the grass. Her heart was burdened by several confusing emotions. She had worked in recovery from drug
addiction for six months, but often she had days when
she felt depressed and wanted to numb her painful
feelings.

She heard the sound of a whistle and looked down to
see a train winding through the valley. The train was
composed of an engine, several freight cars, and a
shiny red caboose.

The train reminded Diane of an example her sponsor had once shared with her. In recovery the engine
that pulls us through is the truthful facts we know.
Those facts need to be followed up by faith that God
will take care of us. The caboose of our healing involves our feelings. Just as the caboose never pulls the
train, we must be careful not to allow our emotions to
lead us.

Diane realized that she had been focusing on her
painful feelings. She took a few moments to remind
herself of the fact that recovery was her only path to a
healthy life and that God would give her the strength
to continue forward.

We move in the right direction when we are led by the facts.

                                                      CSH

Men shall speak of the might of Your awesome acts,
And I will declare Your greatness.   —PS. 145:6

I don't usually chance sharing with people my relationship with God. It's a very personal topic, and perhaps I have feared rejection. I grew up with the idea that it was easier to hold my feelings inside than to risk rejection.

During dinner with two friends, we began talking about religion and faith. I learned one of my friends was agnostic and the other was an atheist. I remember feeling startled. All my life I had operated with the knowledge there was God, who was far more powerful than I. We discussed how they felt and their justifications. Then they asked me why I believed in God. No one had ever asked me that point-blank.

What followed next came as a surprise. I began to talk, but I found myself saying things I had never said to anyone before. Thirty minutes passed, and my companions still listened. They didn't interrupt. The odd thing is, I don't remember what was said.

My friend who was agnostic has since become a Christian. I have no doubt God was with us that night, and I'm sure he remembers what was said.

Even a single candle glows brightly where it is dark (Suzy Blaylock).
BLB

Be still, and know that I am God.
—PS. 46:10

Morning has arrived as I sit on the bank of a small river in the mountains of Tennessee. Even in July the air is cool and crisp.

Close your eyes and join me. Hear the crystal water gurgle and splash as it dances over rocks while running downstream. Birds chirp and sing. Wind rustles through the tree leaves. In the distance a woodpecker taps out a tune. Things are peaceful here. Prayer comes freely.

One of the greatest lessons I have learned in recovery is to be still and quiet. Life is stressful, hectic, and full of distractions, so I must make time to restore my peace of mind. I find serenity when I can sit quietly and focus my mind on God. It seems easier for God to talk with me when I take time to listen.

We can't all rush away for a vacation each time we are stressed, but we can create quiet moments right where we are. We can catch a silent moment before the kids wake up; we can turn off the car radio while driving to work; we can even ask others to manage some of our responsibilities and allow us an occasional afternoon off.

———————————

Being quiet clears our minds and lets us talk with God.

CSH

Philip found Nathanael and said to him, "We have found Him of whom Moses in the law, and also the prophets, wrote—Jesus of Nazareth, the son of Joseph." And Nathanael said to him, "Can anything good come out of Nazareth?" Philip said to him, "Come and see."   —JOHN 1:45–46

God allows us the joy of being fellow laborers with the saints in spreading the gospel and leading others to Christ. How do we go about presenting this message of God's grace convincingly to others when at times we feel confused and inadequate ourselves? Do we work out a plan to the last detail, marking passages in the Bible to show them? Do we swamp them with literature about salvation? Do we pray for guidance from God?

All of the above can be effective witnessing, but we can also say, as Philip said, "Come and see." We can share with others by inviting them to a Twelve-Step meeting. Here they will see for themselves the spiritual awakening that takes place by working the program.

Let's not get so caught up in our presentation of the gospel, our biblical knowledge, or our inadequacies that we don't simply ask those around us to "come and see."

BLB

> [*Peter*] *denied Him, saying, "Woman, I do not*
> *know Him."*
> —LUKE 22:57

When Jesus predicted that Peter would deny him, Peter adamantly proclaimed that he would die before he would ever deny Jesus. Peter's good intentions were shattered that very same night when three times he denied being a follower of Jesus.

After he thought through his denial, Peter wept and was overcome with grief. I imagine that at that moment he felt totally hopeless, and he must have despaired that he would never serve God again. In that time of anguish, he could never have believed that God would choose to use him in the future in mighty ways and would inspire him to write parts of the Bible. It was through God's grace that Peter was restored to fellowship.

Many of us remember a painful time when we felt our lives were worthless and ruined. In Twelve-Step recovery we come to understand our past and we make amends with the people we harmed. We can now encourage people in the program who feel hopeless like Peter.

We are an example of God's gracious ability to restore our relationship with him.

CSH

> *"But he who enters by the door is the shepherd of the sheep. To him the doorkeeper opens, and the sheep hear his voice; and he calls his own sheep by name and leads them out. And when he brings out his own sheep, he goes before them; and the sheep follow him, for they know his voice."*
>
> —JOHN 10:2-4

We often find ourselves in the position of a shepherd. As a parent, teacher, supervisor, scoutmaster, or coach, we find ourselves desiring to influence those around us to accomplish a task or to achieve a greater good. We long to see our children follow a holy and righteous path. We want them to meet with good and not evil. We hope to inspire our children to seek knowledge and truth and to apply it in their lives.

But what about our methods? Do we act as a true shepherd or do we drive as a taskmaster? From John we learn the right method. First, the true shepherd enters by the door and accepts the sheep in an acceptable way. Second, the shepherd calls them by name. Third, the shepherd leads them out, without pushing or pulling. Last, the shepherd goes before them.

Let us be concerned about those God has given us to shepherd (Dick Blaylock).

BLB

> *It is well to give when asked, but it is better to give*
> *unasked, through understanding.*
> —KAHLIL GIBRAN

Elizabeth sat across the group and watched the young woman. She noticed how her hands trembled as she held a tissue. Elizabeth went back in her mind to six years ago when she attended her first AA meeting. She remembered being so nervous that day that she had felt nauseated during group. She offered a prayer of compassion in her heart for this new member who was in such obvious pain.

After the meeting Elizabeth went straight to the new woman and introduced herself. A faint smile traced the tear-stained face of the woman who said her name was Missy. Missy quietly explained that she had just left a detox unit that morning and was feeling very afraid.

Elizabeth sat down with Missy and briefly shared her own story. She encouraged Missy and said that she understood exactly what she was going through. As Missy made a commitment to come to group, Elizabeth felt the joy of knowing she had helped someone begin the journey of recovery.

Reach out with love to lead others toward healing.

CSH

Oh, sing to the LORD a new song!
Sing to the LORD, all the earth.
Sing to the LORD. —PS. 96:1–2

Ron had been persuaded to sing with his company choir at the Christmas tree-lighting ceremony. Nervously he clambered up the risers to face a crowd of several hundred employees. Everyone turned their attention to the festive singers dressed in red and green. The conductor raised his hands. The sound was triumphant, but Ron couldn't hear himself sing. He looked around the group of singers and he looked at the audience, trying desperately to hear himself. Toward the front of the audience was a woman Ron did not know, but she smiled as if she recognized him. She was singing. Near her another began to sing. He couldn't hear them, but he knew they were singing the same song he was singing.

As people tell their stories at Alcoholics Anonymous, others smile and nod, because they too have been up in front of the audience. Now they stand in support of those who try to tell their own story.

From the heart, we all sing the same song (Ronald C. Harris, Jr.).

BLB

> *Jesus . . . said to him, "Go home to your friends,*
> *and tell them what great things the Lord has done*
> *for you, and how He has had compassion on you."*
> —MARK 5:19

A man who was possessed by many demons lived outside the city in the graveyard. No one was able to help this man or control his behavior. He walked among the tombs, screaming and cutting himself.

One day Jesus met this man of the tombs. Jesus commanded all of the demons to leave. After the demons departed, the man became calm and sane. He had a great love for Jesus because Jesus had set him free from the torment he had suffered for years.

As Jesus prepared to leave, the man pleaded to go with him. Jesus asked him to stay and tell others of the miraculous healing that took place in his life.

Once we are set free from our bondage to addictions, we often want to isolate ourselves and spend all our time meditating on God's Word. We need to go out and share the good news with others.

Silence about recovery won't benefit anyone.

CSH

*The woman then left her waterpot, went her way
into the city, and said to the men, "Come, see a
Man who told me all things that I ever did. Could
this be the Christ?"*
—JOHN 4:28–29

Dick remembered that, as a child at Christmas, he
rushed out to the den to find toys and gifts under the
tree. After tearing apart the packages and discovering
what was inside, he wanted to call his best friend to tell
him the good news about his gifts.

Dick is married now. When his daughter Sara was
born, he rushed out of the delivery room to announce
to family and friends the good news. With a pocketful
of quarters, he spent the morning on the phone calling
his friends.

God has given us the greatest gift of all, salvation
through his Son, Jesus Christ. Upon receiving this most
precious of all gifts, have we rushed out to tell others?
This book is my way of sharing the miracle of love and
forgiveness, reclaimed and accepted, through a
Twelve-Step program.

*Let's become more like the Samaritan woman who ran to tell others
about Christ.*

BLB

About the Authors

Cynthia Spell Humbert is a member of the professional staff of the Minirth-Meier Clinic in Dallas, Texas, where she has an active outpatient practice. Her clinical experience includes group, marriage, family, and individual therapy.

Cynthia has a Master of Science degree in counseling psychology from Georgia State University and a Master's in Christian counseling from Psychological Studies Institute in Atlanta, Georgia.

She has led seminars on codependency, building self-esteem, post-abortion trauma, and incest recovery. Cynthia appears on ACT's television program "COPE," and is often a guest on the national radio call-in program "The Minirth-Meier Clinic."

Cynthia lives with her husband, David, in Plano, Texas.

Betty Lively Blaylock is a licensed professional counselor with the Minirth-Meier Clinic in Dallas, Texas. She received her Doctorate in guidance and counseling from Western Colorado University after completing her Bachelor's and Master's degrees from Southern Methodist University in Dallas.

A member of the Texas Association for Children of Alcoholics, Dr. Blaylock has extensive experience counseling adult children of alcoholics. She has worked as a collegiate academic advisor and teacher, helping students face, often for the first time, issues of sex, drugs, alcohol, and eating disorders.

Dr. Blaylock and her husband, Charles, are parents and grandparents and live in north Dallas.

Frank L. Minirth, M.D., is a cofounder of the Minirth-Meier Clinic in Dallas, Texas, one of the largest psychiatric clinics in the United States. He is a diplomate of the American Board of Psychiatry and Neurology and received his M.D. degree from the University of Arkansas College of Medicine. Dr. Minirth is co-author of more than thirty books.

Dr. Minirth lives with his wife, Mary Alice, in the Dallas area.